The Common Core Guidebook™:
Informational Text Lessons 3-5

Rozlyn Linder

Guided Practice, Suggested Book Lists, and Reproducible Organizers

The Common Core Guidebook™, 3-5: INFORMATIONAL TEXT LESSONS

Guided Practice, Suggested Book Lists, and Reproducible Organizers

Rozlyn Linder, Ph.D.

The Literacy Initiative
Atlanta

The Common Core Guidebook™, 3-5: Informational Text Lessons
www.CommonCoreGuidebook.com

THE COMMON CORE GUIDEBOOK is a trademark of The Literacy Initiative, LLC.
541 Tenth Street Suite 258, Atlanta, Georgia 30318

Cover and Interior Design: Buzz Branding, LLC.

Library of Congress Cataloging-in-Publication Data
CIP data is on file with the Library of Congress.
ISBN: 978-0-9889505-3-5

Printed in the U. S. A.

For Sydney and Brooke

CONTENTS

CONTENTS

ORGANIZATION OF THIS BOOK

This book is organized to provide guidance for explicit skill instruction for each element of the Common Core informational text reading standards. Each element relies on strong teacher background knowledge, introduction of skills through accessible, real-world understandings, think-aloud modeling by the teacher, guided-practice opportunities, and finally individual application of the strategies with independent texts. *The Common Core Guidebook* is not a replacement for your curriculum. It is, however, a framework of strategies and resources to support the understanding of the informational text reading standards.

THEORETICAL FRAMEWORK

This book relies on the *gradual release* model of reading instruction (Pearson & Gallagher, 1983). Derived from a model used for comprehension strategies, this approach offers a reliable instructional routine that scaffolds and provides support for skill development. The responsibility for the use of a strategy transfers from the teacher to collaborative, and eventually to independent, application.

Each skill should be explicitly introduced by the teacher, with most of the initial accountability lying with the teacher. Think-aloud modeling is where the teacher begins to show students the process that he or she uses to make sense of text and implement the specific skill. The practice opportunities are developed so that teachers can offer joint responsibility through collaborative and guided practice and eventually release the full responsibility to the students. Each section of this book, guided by the literacy research on the gradual release model, is a critical component to delivering your instruction of the Common Core informational text standards. There is one chapter for each standard.

Each chapter is organized into four components:

- ▶ **Understand the Standard**
- ▶ **Introduce the Standard**
- ▶ **Think-Aloud Modeling with the Standard**
- ▶ **Practice the Standard**

UNDERSTAND THE STANDARD

This is about you, as a teacher, making sure that you have expert knowledge of the standard. *What key skills do students need? What essential knowledge is critical?* You are positioning yourself as an expert. This is the section of the book that gives you the guidance and background to confirm your understanding of each element of the standard. Research indicates that alignment between instruction and standards is often weak (Polikoff, 2012; Spillane, 2004). Your understanding of the standards is a key variable to effectively impacting student achievement.

INTRODUCE THE STANDARD

This section is where you take the core elements of the standard and connect them with your kids. Independent of any text, this is your chance to make connections with the skill they will be learning and their real lives. You want to think outside of the box and find a way to explain the core of the concept in relationship to what matters to them or what they already understand and can make sense of. Your goal is to make the learning concrete and relevant. Vygotsky (1978) asserts that all learning goes from concrete to abstract. This section is where you are attempting to reach an access point from which all kids can build a concrete foundation, regardless of reading levels or ability. This is the anticipatory element that frames the learning from a nonthreatening angle. You are simply making sense of the skill in a way that is concrete and clear. You will note that this section is the most social and relies on high levels of interaction between you and your students.

THINK-ALOUD MODELING WITH THE STANDARD

Think-aloud modeling is the core of the instruction. Now that you have made a connection between the skill and more accessible knowledge, you are going to think-aloud to model how you would use the skills embedded in each standard to make meaning of text. There are two bodies of research from which this section draws. First is the data on the effectiveness of modeling for students; the second is the empirical evidence on the value of the think-aloud protocol.

Modeling for students is an explicit component of scaffolding instruction. This is essential across any content area. You will find that modeling is particularly important for struggling readers who have yet to connect the skills with the process of application.

Research Based

If teachers provide modeling, with a clear purpose, learning occurs.

(Hinchman & Sheridan- Thomas, 2008)

Think-aloud modeling is where the teacher actually lets students see the process that we, as adults, use to make sense of text and implement the specific skills. While no one can capture all of the inner workings of the mind, the think-aloud offers students a snapshot of the mind's eye. The think-aloud helps demonstrate the cognitive process (Davey, 1983). This explicit moment creates a map of the interpretive road upon which a reader travels to make meaning. Effective teachers talk about their thinking as they do it.

An extension to this strategy is to invite students to think-aloud with you. This places value on how readers can verbalize and think about text. You want to guide students through your thought process and invite them to consider their own. Modeling your thinking and asking students to do the same is a process that helps students to enhance their own self-monitoring abilities (Baumann, Jones, & Seifert-

Kessel, 1993). Students become partners with you as you walk them through your own navigational methods for using the strategies embedded in the standard to negotiate textual meaning. This process leads to better discussions about text and a more thorough understanding of text (Oster, 2001). As a teacher, I want students to repeatedly hear how I navigate text and apply strategies.

PRACTICE THE STANDARD

The *Practice the Standard* section has ready-to-use graphic organizers that can extend learning through formative assessment, guided practice, and independent practice.

FORMATIVE ASSESSMENT

Formative assessments are ongoing evaluations and observations of student understanding (Fisher & Frey, 2007). These assessments differ from assessments *of* learning and are really assessments *for* learning. These are practice opportunities for students to apply the skills and strategies that they have developed to independent or guided tasks. The graphic organizers included in this book can be used as formative assessments for student learning. Remember that formative assessments do not need to be graded and are used to inform you of where your students are. This information should help you make decisions about where to go next with your instructional plan. *Do you need to reteach? How differentiated should your lessons be? Should you scaffold and release responsibility to students at a slower or faster pace?* These questions are answered by frequent and consistent formative assessment opportunities. These organizers are lucid opportunities to do just that and support the learning process.

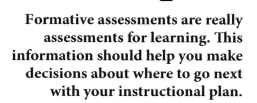

Key Point

Formative assessments are really assessments for learning. This information should help you make decisions about where to go next with your instructional plan.

When you use the organizers as formative assessments, be careful to consider what comes next. Assessments should drive your future instruction and inform students of their progress. Assessing and looking at learning can and should be a collaborative process. This means that you need to have conversations, ask students to consider their own metacognition, and share their thoughts about what they are doing and how they make sense of the text. You want to help students not just look for their understandings, but to catch misunderstandings along the way. Teachers need to aggressively check for understanding and make sure that students have a chance to 'get it' before it is too late (Wiggins, 2005).

GUIDED PRACTICE

As you observe and collect data on your students, you will notice that many need additional support. This is when you use the organizers to guide their practice and reteach. This can be organized in several different ways: small group, one-on-one, or in pairs. I like to group students who have demonstrated similar understandings (or misunderstandings) together and work with them through teacher-driven guided practice. Talking with readers about what they are doing or where they are getting confused in order to offer strategies and redirection is crucial. Guided practice provides an up-close opportunity to scaffold instruction and provide substantive feedback (Almasi & Fullerton, 2012). Each standard in this book has an organizer completed through guided practice based on exemplars listed in the Common Core appendices (National Governors Association Center & Council of Chief State School Officers, 2010) or news articles. The same text was selected for consistent models within each standard. Walking students through those examples and helping them to apply the strategies to other informational text is an appropriate way to scaffold and offer support for students.

Independent Practice

As students begin to build their knowledge base, the key with the Common Core standards is to ensure that students continue to refine and practice the skills that they have learned. There are multiple ways to do this. The organizers can be assigned as homework, serve as classroom activities, or become standing practice opportunities in literacy centers or stations. Students can select organizers that they find demonstrate their own learning or meet the purpose of a larger assignment. Many schools rely on reading incentive programs where students take multiple-choice tests on the computer or through their media centers. I encourage teachers to have students use an organizer to practice or reinforce a skill along with the basic recall test that many of these programs use. Pair the skill-based practice with the assessment; this encourages students to use a much more critical eye and extend their thinking in ways that a knowledge-level quiz simply cannot. The variations of methods for using the organizers to meet students' needs are endless.

Suggested Book Lists

A central demand of the Common Core State Standards is that readers navigate texts of increasing complexity. This is actually standard number ten for all grade levels. While this is not tied to a specific lesson that you will teach your students, it is a factor that you, as the teacher, need to be aware of. Text complexity levels should influence your text choices for assignments, modeling, or even suggested reading within your classroom. To help support your instructional decision making, each chapter, organized by standard, includes a list of suggested texts. These texts represent specific readings that reinforce the skills necessary for mastery of the standard. Many of the choices are digital, while others are print. As you consider which books to use with your students, it is important to note that the Common Core State Standards have established a three-part model to help teachers make decisions about text. The expectation is that teachers consider three different measures: qualitative, quantitative, and reader/task. Each component is weighted

Key Point

As you consider which books to use with your students, it is important to note that the Common Core State Standards have established a three-part model to help teachers make decisions about text. The expectation is that teachers consider three different measures: qualitative, quantitative, and reader/task.

equally and should guide teachers to select model texts that fit the needs of their students. Appendix A of the Common Core State Standards includes 43 pages about why text complexity is such a strong focus and how to determine and measure text complexity. You can find this document here: http://www.corestandards.org/assets/Appendix_A.pdf.

QUALITATIVE MEASURES

Qualitative factors can only be measured by a human. This is not a number, or a figure computed by a book company. Qualitative measures include determinations of the structure, knowledge demands, dimensions, and language conventionality. This measure is about examining the text for **meaning.** *Are there multiple levels of meaning? Is the meaning hidden or obscure?* Teachers also look for **structure.** This is about the organization patterns, genre, and physical features of the text. Finally, **language demands** are considered. *How much domain-specific vocabulary is used? Is the language figurative or complex?* Many districts have scales to guide teachers in determining the qualitative appropriateness of text.

QUANTITATIVE MEASURES

Quantitative factors consider word and sentence length and frequency. These measures are typically based on algorithms and measured by software. Because a number is much simpler to latch onto, many districts and teachers often use this as their only guide when selecting text. I strongly advise against this. This is just one-third of the text-complexity puzzle. There are numerous companies and leveling systems that can meet this quantitative need. Fountas and Pinnell have a guided-reading leveling system that I have used for over a decade to determine the level of different types of books. The Flesch-Kincaid Grade Level Readability Scale is one of the most transparent and widely available free calculators that provide a grade-level equivalent for text. The Developmental Reading Assessment® (DRA) has a leveling system that provides numeric representations of the reading level of different books. I am sure that there are a wide variety of additional options that exist.

Key Point

At the time of this publication, the Lexile® measure was becoming one of the most prevalent forms of book leveling. In response, I have included the Lexile® measure for each book on the suggested text list for each standard.

At the time of this publication, the Lexile® measure was becoming one of the most prevalent and consistently referred-to forms of book leveling. The Lexile® measure is a copyrighted book leveling indicator created by the MetaMetrics Company. In response, I have included the Lexile® measure for each book on the suggested text list for each standard. This is not an endorsement of this system of leveling, but rather an attempt to be responsive to a measure that many teachers and schools look for.

READER/TASK MEASURES

Teacher professional judgment informs how this component is measured. First, teachers consider the tasks that students will complete with the text. Based on the activities, certain types of text may be more appropriate than others. This is an opportunity to determine how aligned the text is with the learning or assignment. The second step is really about knowing your readers. Considerations of experiences, background knowledge, and motivation should be a focus here. This might cause a text with high-interest content and a quantitative score that is typically considered too high for your readers to be selected. It might also allow for a text that has a lower quantitative score to be selected for precise alignment to the topic being studied, experiences, or interests.

Throughout *The Common Core Guidebook*, you will notice different signs and symbols. These signposts are there to point out or reinforce important information.

This symbol indicates some Common Core terminology that students will hear and read often in the standards.

This icon indicates a link to the writing standards.

These are key ideas to reinforce that are central to your instruction. Don't forget these tips and pointers!

Here you'll discover what the empirical evidence or research says about specific practices or strategies.

Watch out! When you see this symbol, you will get some advice about what to avoid or be careful of in your classroom.

Here are some ways to extend students' thinking or differentiate instruction.

THE NEW SHINY PRETTY

Every so many years, there seems to be some shift in education. The pattern is inevitably uniform each time.

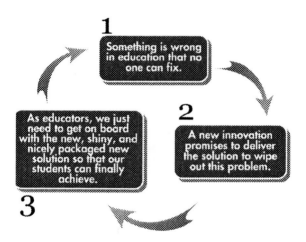

This is the phenomenon that I have dubbed: *The New Shiny Pretty*. In almost two decades as a public school educator, I have seen new instructional reform models, new standards, and shifts in assessments numerous times. Each time, a new focus is lauded as the great savior of education. In fact, I have gotten pretty good at reading through the rhetoric and sorting out exactly what is usually just a new name for an old idea. I am used to shuffling what I already do around and renaming it whatever *The New Shiny Pretty* has determined is the new title for what we are already doing.

My natural inclination when I first heard about the new Common Core standards was to assume that it was time for the latest and greatest *New Shiny*

Pretty and that this was it. I resisted doing much more than printing out the standards and reading over them a few times. As a veteran teacher, this seemed like what I already did. Honestly, how much can reading change? It is always about reading, writing, and language. *The New Shiny Pretty* might label the parts differently, but the parts are still the same. As I began my usual process of sorting out where the new and old lined up, I kept coming to roadblocks. Some of the skills that had persevered through other reforms seemed to be missing. Some of the new skills used language that I had only seen in my college classes. These Common Core standards were not what I thought they would be. The standards required a different mindset, a new way of looking at literacy for educators, and a new set of strategies. Something was amiss with this *New Shiny Pretty*. It didn't just seem to shine things up and repackage them. This was, dare I say it, *different.* My theory about nothing being new in education was tossed on its backside.

Checklist Teaching

Whether it is because of increased accountability or the rise in high-stakes testing, what we, as teachers, have gotten very good at is the Checklist Method of teaching. We simply check off behaviors that are associated with literacy. For example, if successful readers should be able to recognize cause/effect relationships, we teach our students how to recognize a cause/effect relationship and test to see if they can do it. When we finish that, we move on to other indicators of literacy. At the end of our units, we expect students to *apply* these skills. Often the application is in the form of a multiple choice test where students use skills like cause/effect, sequencing, or drawing conclusions to pick the correct answer from a set of four choices about a text. This is how we have taught literacy for a while. Students in third grade do it this way. Students in eighth grade do it this way. High school seniors do it this way. Those who can select the correct response have mastered skills. Unfortunately these students go off to college and are asked to analyze text and write about it. This is when the hammer drops; they cannot do it.

Research Based

Teaching skills and standards has to become recursive. Understanding that skills can be applied to multiple texts and opportunities to practice this application are key. Developing critical-thinking skills and an awareness of what to do when they encounter informational text is crucial.

"Let students read frequently. Holding students back because they have not mastered all of the requisite skills is ineffective. Give students the skills, but let them practice and hone those skills with books. Students need multiple opportunities to engage with text to grow as readers."

(Anderson, Wilson, and Fielding, 1995)

Just Play Tennis

Understanding how the Common Core standards differ from what teachers have primarily done in the past requires a new way of looking at literacy. The Common Core standards do not expect students to only demonstrate mastery of skills in isolation. The Common Core informational text standards demand that students continuously perform skills in concert, with an eye on recursive practice and mastery.

A great analogy to understand this shift in thinking is to compare Common Core literacy to playing a sport. An individual sport like golf or tennis is a perfect comparison. The students are playing a game of their own; they are "doing literacy." Just as Serena Williams or Gabby Douglas must use multiple skills, techniques, and strategies in their sports, so do our students.

Compare the training that Serena Williams has to the average ALTA tennis player. If they learned to play tennis under the Checklist Method of teaching skills and testing them, both Serena and the ALTA player would have been identified as masters of the sport. Do they both know how to serve? Check. Do they both know how to volley? Check. Do they both know the rules of the game? Check. Do they both understand how to hit backhands? Check.

Common Core literacy is the opposite of Checklist teaching.

Under the Checklist Method, both are adequate tennis players. In reality, Serena and the average ALTA player could hardly even play a game together. It would be a shutout. I imagine that Serena's serves would probably never even be returned. So . . . what went wrong? They both learned the same skills. We checked them off. We are sure that they mastered the skills. What exactly happened? This is the same thing that happens in classrooms. Teachers are teaching skills, checking for understanding, and moving on to their other (typically state-mandated) requirements for instruction. The teaching is not the problem. The problem is that the Checklist Method does not produce tennis players. It produces people who can demonstrate skills related to tennis, but cannot use them in concert or independently. This is the same in the classroom. The Checklist Method does not result in students who can "do literacy." It produces people who know something about literacy and literacy-related behaviors. Despite this knowledge they can't "do literacy."

Often students are held back from progressing to more complex, higher-level skills until they master previous skills. With the Common Core standards students will have explicit skill instruction, but continue to perfect those skills as they are introduced to others. Consider the tennis analogy again here. You don't move to the backhand once your forehand is perfect. If that was the case, you would never get to the backhand. You aren't forbidden to serve if you cannot volley. Imagine if that was how you learned to play tennis. When would you get to play in a game? We have to get students out on the court and let them play the game, observe them so we can offer feedback, and coach them on their weaknesses. Students cannot wait to "do literacy" until they have all the skills perfected. They have to practice "doing literacy" on concrete, on courts with tattered nets, on indoor courts, in bad weather, on hot days, and when it is a bit chilly. If they just work on skills and never use them in concert independently, when they have to play the game — they won't be able to.

"The more experiences and time spent with text, the more marked the reading achievement gains are."

(National Institute of Child Health and Human Development, 2000)

DECONSTRUCTING TEXT

"Doing literacy" is something that schools have rarely done well consistently. In fact, I am not sure if we have ever truly taught students to "do literacy." This is one of the major shifts that Common Core suggests. What Common Core proposes is that teachers abandon the Checklist Method of instruction and teach students to do ONE thing. That is not an error; you did not read the text wrong. You teach students one thing under Common Core. You don't teach reading, writing, comprehension, or grammar. Common Core literacy teachers are only tasked with teaching one thing:

We teach students to independently deconstruct text and communicate about it.

Key Point

As students move to the college level, this deconstruction evolves into what traditionally has been described as rhetorical analysis. The language and the descriptors may change, but the core is the same: text deconstruction. Text means images, digital media, and print. How do students take apart text? This is what we want to explicitly teach them how to do so that they can apply it to varying types of text. Many people struggle with this because they want to center their instruction on a particular author or genre. Those things are fine, but they are not the *purpose,* they are the *tools.* The focus is on taking apart text. Students learn to take apart text and use those same skills when they encounter new and unfamiliar text.

The more students spend time actually reading and "doing literacy", the more they develop fluency, linguistic competence, and confidence *(Caldwell & Gaine, 2000).* **The more you put them on the court, the better they are at the sport.**

THE ELEMENTARY SCHOOL STANDARDS

Theoretically, moving away from being a Checklist Teacher to teaching text deconstruction is the most critical step for Common Core teachers. To make this a reality, teachers need a strong understanding of what they have to actually teach in the classroom. When I first began to get ready to bring the Common Core standards into my classroom, I read everything I could get my hands on. The more I read, the more convoluted the standards seemed. Well, luckily for all of us, Common Core is actually a nice tidy list that makes sense—you just need the right lens to rip away all of the "extra" stuff and focus on the standards. That is precisely what *The Common Core Guidebook* does. When you teach students about informational text, you are only teaching NINE

Research Based

"... we need to consider the multiple and overlapping forms of literacy, including digital, visual, spoken, and printed forms that require the reader to critically analyze, deconstruct, and reconstruct meaning across a variety of texts for various purposes."

(Mandel Morrow, Gambrell, & Duke, p. 48)

standards. Consider these to be your **RI (Reading Informational Text) Standards.**

RI 1.   **TEXTUAL EVIDENCE**

RI 2.   **MAIN IDEA**

RI 3.   **EVENTS & CONCEPTS**

RI 4.   **WORD PLAY**

RI 5.   **TEXT STRUCTURE**

RI 6.   **POINT OF VIEW**

RI 7.   **BEYOND TEXT**

RI 8.   **EVIDENCE & CONNECTIONS**

RI 9.   **MULTIPLE SOURCES**

You may notice that standard ten is missing. That is intentional. Standard ten reads as:

3rd: By the end of the year, read and comprehend informational texts, including history/social studies, science, and technical texts, in the grades 2-3 text complexity band independently and proficiently.

4th: By the end of the year, read and comprehend informational texts, including history/social studies, science, and technical texts, in the grades 4-5 text complexity band proficiently, with scaffolding as needed at the high end of the range.

5th: By the end of the year, read and comprehend informational texts, including history/ social studies, science, and technical texts, in the grades 4-5 text complexity band independently and proficiently.

Key Point

(RI) Standard ten is a *teacher standard*, not a student standard.

This is a standard for the teacher, not the students. Your students are not trying to prove to you that they are reading increasingly complex text throughout the year. That is your job. You are in charge of suggesting texts and introducing them. Don't make that a student standard; teach the other standards and provide varying texts throughout the ten months that you have your students.

14

Textual Evidence

"A fact in itself is nothing. It is valuable only for the idea attached to it, or for the proof which it furnishes."
Claude Bernard, *physiologist*

READING INFORMATIONAL TEXT STANDARD 1:
TEXTUAL EVIDENCE

Third	Fourth	Fifth
Ask and answer questions to demonstrate understanding of a text, referring explicitly to the text as the basis for the answers.	Refer to details and examples in a text when explaining what the text says explicitly and when drawing inferences from the text.	Quote accurately from a text when explaining what the text says explicitly and when drawing inferences from the text.

GRADE LEVEL DIFFERENCES

Students in each grade are tasked with explicitly referencing the text. Third graders are only responsible for providing textual evidence in response to questions about a text or when asking their own questions. This means that your traditional 5Ws are now extended to ask for textual evidence to support responses instead of just asking for a response. In fourth grade, students are asked to use textual evidence to support explicit and inferential statements about the text. Finally, in fifth grade, students will do exactly the same thing, but they should be able to quote the passage, excerpt, or sentence when making their inferences. This represents a logical cognitive progression.

16

The *Textual Evidence* standard is the foundation upon which all of the other standards are built. Most of the informational text that students encounter in grades 3-5 will present an argument or inform the reader. This type of informational writing relies heavily on evidence.

So, what exactly is textual evidence? Textual evidence is **support lifted directly from the text to support inferences, claims, and questions.** The Textual Evidence standard demands that readers engage with the text and share what specific aspects of the text influence their thinking and help them to make meaning of the text or prompt them to consider ideas or additional questions.

Third Grade

You will note that the language of the third-grade standard states that students should ask and answer questions to demonstrate understanding of the text. This does not mean that they should reply to a set of ready-made questions to meet the rigor of the standard. What it does mean is that students can reply to questions, ask their own questions, and identify what specific areas of the passage helped them to answer the question or prompted them to ask the question. A good practice is to have students *question* the text *as they read.* What questions arise? When they finish the text, what questions do they now have? Students should question and wonder about text and be able to point to textual evidence that prompted those ques-

Key Point

"Inferring is the bedrock of comprehension, not only in reading. We infer in many realms. Our life clicks along more smoothly if we can read the world as well as text."

(Harvey & Goudvis, 2000, p. 105)

tions. Teaching students to **consider questions** and **challenge assumptions** is critical. If they annotate as they read, they are able to mark or use sticky notes to indicate the textual evidence that prompted their questions.

Fourth and Fifth Grade

When planning instruction for this standard, it is important to note a difference: third graders just need to reference the text. Fourth and fifth graders need the text-reference component to support *inferences* as well.

There are two different types of things that anyone can say after reading a text. One is that they noticed something that was **explicit.** These are those things that are stated directly in the text. For example: *Oprah Winfrey is very wealthy.* If the text spells that information out for the reader, it is explicit; the textual evidence is the actual statement. The other types of things that we notice are **implicit.** We make meaning based on clues from the text. These are *inferences.* Students need direct textual evidence to support inferences. *Oprah Winfrey is a hard worker.* This could be an example of an inference that a student might make after reading a biography or article about Winfrey's life. The text may never state explicitly that she was a hard worker, but specific lines of text might support this inference.

Many materials or lesson ideas call for students to explain the explicit meaning of a text and point to textual evidence. That is appropriate for third graders only. To meet the rigor of this standard in fourth and fifth grade, students have to make an inference, determine what textual evidence supports it, and refer to it (fourth grade) or quote it (fifth grade).

1 **Show your students photographs of people with different expressions.** I find that the best source for this is to simply search images using Bing or Google for "sad person," "happy person," "angry person," etc. *"Let's look at a photograph together."* Show students one image at a time and ask them to think about who is in the picture and how they feel. You may even consider writing down questions to guide their thinking. *Who? What? When? Where?* Call on multiple students to share their ideas about the photograph. Jot down the thoughts on chart paper, recording the student who shared the thought next to their idea.

2 **Discuss the comments that the students shared about the photographs.** *"You guys shared some great thoughts about these images. I do have one more question about these photographs."* Write on the board: How do you know? *"You guys seem to know a lot about these pictures! I am curious about how you know these things. How do you know?"* Call on students to share the evidence or clues from the images that led to their decisions about the photographs. Be sure to point out that we make decisions about the world around us based on evidence. *"Let's try this activity again, but use a book instead of photographs."*

3 **Select an informational text that you can read aloud with your students.** Make sure that students have their own copies of the text. This is a great time to turn to your science or social studies text when introducing this part of the lesson. If you have a book that you don't have multiple copies of, use a document camera or photocopy a few pages so that students can have the same text in front of them.

4 **Explain that when people make decisions, based on evidence, those decisions are called inferences.** *"As we read, I want you to make some decisions, or inferences, about this text. This is the exact same thing that we just did with the photographs."*

5 **After you read the text, call on students to share inferences and the supporting textual evidence.** Create a chart to display these inferences. Instead of creating a new chart for each book we read, I like to make one anchor chart and have students record their inferences on large sticky notes that we can remove as needed.

6 **Repeat with different parts of the book or other books as needed.**

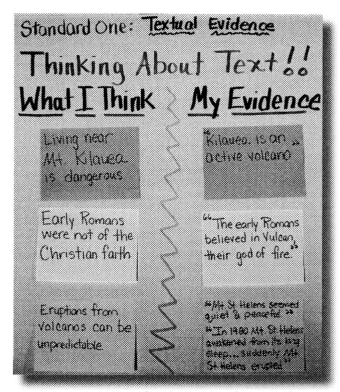

Textual Evidence anchor chart created using
Volcanoes *by Seymour Simon.*

18

1   **Select a short informational text excerpt.** I like to use short pieces that feature content that my students are interested in and encourage high levels of engagement. This selection could come from the suggested list at the end of this chapter or your own collection.

2   **Explain that our decisions about a text should be based on evidence from that text.** "*You cannot just say that a text is about the importance of brushing your teeth if you cannot prove it. I cannot say that a text is about how easy it is to draw Spider-Man if I cannot show you what in the text helped me to make that decision. Today I am going to show you very clearly how I think about a text and support my thoughts with evidence.*"

3   "*I am going to use a sentence frame to think about text.*" On the board, or on a chart, write: I THINK_____. THE TEXTUAL EVIDENCE THAT SUPPORTS MY THINKING IS_____. THE AUTHOR WROTE _____. THIS HELPED _____. "*As I read this text, I am going to stop when I have some ideas, inferences, or decisions about the text. But I won't stop there. I am going to show you what in the text helped me to make that decision.*"

4   **Read the text aloud with students.** Make sure that students have a copy of the text or can clearly view the words on a projector. As you read out loud, stop frequently to fill in your sentence frame and demonstrate your thought process.

5   **Repeat this activity with multiple excerpts.** You really want students to have at least 2-3 sentence frames that they have seen you make and think through. Teaching students to make inferences requires repeated modeling (Zweirs, 2010). The anchor chart here was completed collaboratively. As I read the text, one student provided an inference which she wrote on a large sticky note and added it to the chart. Together, we completed the rest of the sentence frame to document our thinking.

Textual Evidence Sentence Frames

I think [The earthquake helped make the mountain crack more.]. The textual evidence that supports my thinking is [from paragraph one]. The author(s) wrote [Each day brought further quakes." "The mountain began to swell up and crack."]. This helped [a sequence of events] [to show the relationship between more quakes+cracking] [by showing cause and effect]

I used large sticky notes so that we could pull them off and reuse the chart.

THE ORGANIZERS

After you have explicitly introduced and modeled how to apply the strategies of this standard to text, you want to provide students with an organizer that they can use to think about their own informational text reading. In order to make sure that students can independently understand and use the organizer, it is important to model how the specific organizer is used. Select a text and organizer of your choice. Complete the organizer with your students and post it as a model. Afterwards, students can independently use that same organizer multiple times to practice the skill with different informational texts. This can be done in pairs, groups, and independently.

The book that I use with each organizer in this chapter is *Toys! Amazing Stories Behind Some Great Inventions* by Donald Wulffson. This book is used for each example for this standard for consistency and to offer the same book as a point of comparison for teachers.

1 Read (or reread) at least one section from *Toys! Amazing Stories Behind Some Great Inventions*. If you don't have a copy for each student, project the text or use a document camera so that students can follow along and read it. As you talk with your students, be sure to use the language of this standard. Think out loud and complete the organizer together.

2 Once you model by explicitly completing the organizer, your students will understand the connection between the standard and the organizer. You can provide blank copies of the organizer and allow students to select their own informational text, assign one from your class anthology, or select a title from the suggested book list within this chapter.

3 Students can complete an organizer when they read any informational text. This can be done as an assignment and can be repeated as many times as you want with any informational text that you choose. The sky is the limit! This allows for multiple opportunities to tailor the text to the student and maintain fidelity to the standard.

4 Once students have demonstrated mastery of the skill, don't stop using it. You want your readers to keep practicing. In the introduction of the book, I discussed the pitfalls of being a Checklist Teacher. Students need to keep perfecting their skill sets.

5 Reuse the same organizer, make it into an anchor chart, or post exemplars for students to reference later. You can add the organizer to a standards-based center, pair it with your school's reading incentive program, or use it daily as evidence of reading.

ANSWERING QUESTIONS

Common Core
Buzzword

Use the vocabulary of the standard so that students understand the difference between <u>explicit</u> and <u>inference.</u>

Answering Questions

My Inference	Textual Evidence	What Questions Does This Answer?
Toys are often created for other purposes. They are "accidently" turned into toys.	<u>Pg.102-103</u> Play-Doh is made to clean dirty wallpaper. When no one buys it, the inventor gives it to his teacher sister. It becomes a toy! <u>Pg.58</u> Remote-controlled toys began as weapons of war.	How are some toys created? Why do people make toys?

Short on copies? This is one of the easiest for students to recreate on their own.

This works well when looking for multiple pieces of text to support a single inference.

Answering Questions

My Inference	Textual Evidence	What Questions Does This Answer?

QUOTE IT!

This organizer works well with fifth graders who need to quote specific sentences from text.

This is such a good opportunity to teach about ellipses. Students will be able to use them to gather quotes quickly in their notes across all content areas. This is a tool they will continue to use.

| Quote It! | Text: **Toys!** By: **Don Wulffson** |

Page: 28

"The Chinese invented playing cards about a thousand years ago. "

⬇

Card games have been around for a very long time and in faraway places.

Page: 58

"Remote-controlled toys had their beginnings as weapons of war "

⬇

Some toys originally had other purposes.

Page: 102

"...Joe concocted a puttylike substance ... but sales were slow... people weren't interested "

⬇

Sometimes a mistake or a failure can turn into something really good.

I like for students to complete this organizer to prepare for a book talk and use it to discuss the text.

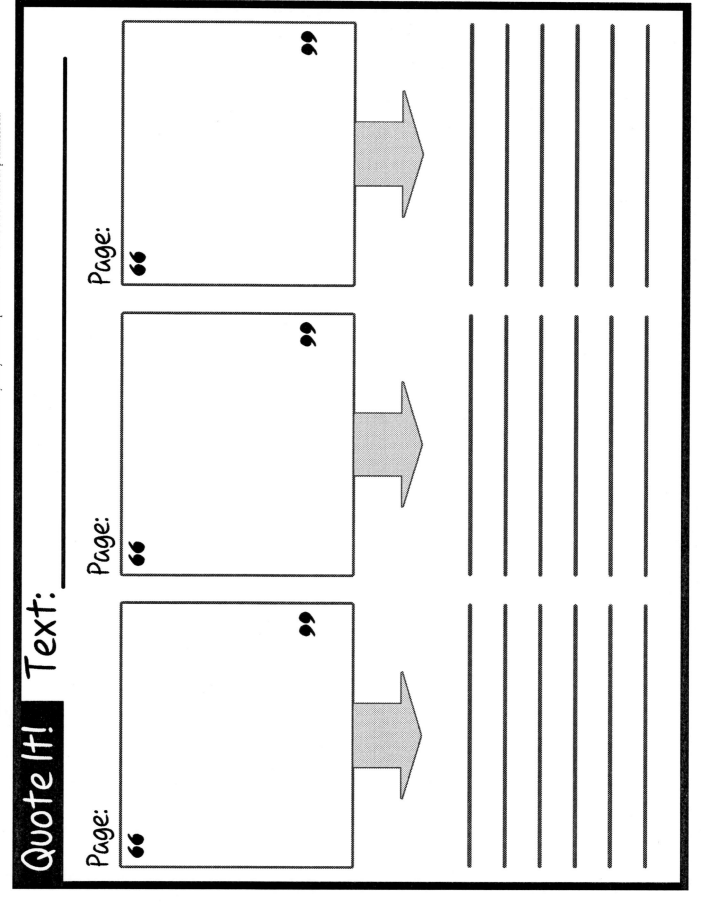

Quote It!

Text: _____

Page:

""   ""

Page:

""   ""

Page:

""   ""

THINKING ABOUT TEXT

24

This is an excellent activity to jigsaw. You can also let students complete what they notice on one side and switch papers to allow different students to look for the textual evidence to support the observations.

Great opportunity to talk about words we use to name text and the components that create larger chunks of text like sentences, lines, and paragraphs.

Thinking About Text

What Do I Think?

Toys have been important to <u>cultures</u> throughout history.

Many toys were really invented by accident & used for other purposes.

How do I Know?

<u>Pg. 83</u> "Even the pharaohs were known to enjoy checkers"

<u>Pg. 69</u> "Czar Peter II of Russia had a very large set of toy soldiers made..."

<u>Pg. 33-37</u> Silly Putty was made by a chemical company looking for a rubber substitute.

<u>Pg. 3</u> Play-Doh was for cleaning wallpaper.

Extend the
Thinking

An alternative is to read a selection and have your students complete colored sticky notes for what they notice. Then, use a different color sticky note for the textual evidence. Use a large wall or table and let students negotiate how the evidence and inferences fit together.

Thinking About Text

How do I Know?

What Do I Think?

TEXTUAL EVIDENCE T-CHART

I like to use this as a quick formative assessment. A sheet of paper folded in half is a quick way for students to write their inferences and identify the textual evidence that supports them.

Students have opportunity and space to include longer excerpts and quote text directly. The fifth-grade standard specifically asks that the students quote text.

Textual Evidence T-Chart

Inference	Textual Evidence
Alot of toys were mistakenly created.	Pg. 5 "It was a mistake. A goof-up."
Some toys were originally dangerous or used as weapons.	Pg. 33 "In 1942... the military turned to the GE company for an answer..."
Toys have been played with for 1000s of years in areas all over the world.	Pg. 19 "People have been doing it for thousands of years..." Pg. 41 "In 1509..." Pg. 45 "In the 15th century..."

Text: __Volcanoes__

Consider assigning text excerpts and asking students to infer from those.

Textual Evidence T-Chart

Inference	Textual Evidence

Text: _____

BIOGRAPHY/ AUTOBIOGRAPHY/ MEMOIR

Amelia to Zora
Cynthia Chin-Lee
1040L
ISBN: 978-1570915239

This 32-page book features one-page biographies of 26 different women. Each biography is organized alphabetically by first name. Some of the women included are: Lena Horne, Jane Goodall, Kristi Yamaguchi, Oprah Winfrey, and Mother Teresa. Illustrations and paintings are found throughout the book. Readers are able to draw inferences about each woman and point to supporting textual evidence for their choices.

Childhood of Famous Americans Series

This series of books features the early years of a wide variety of famous Americans. The books do include some fictionalized details, but are engaging choices for young readers. I find that this series works best with third and fourth graders. These books work particularly well when teaching students to look for main ideas and connections across events, ideas, and people. Listed below are some of the more popular biographies published through this series, along with the ISBN and Lexile level. These books work particularly well with the Textual Evidence, Main Idea, and Events and Concepts standards.

- *Abigail Adams, 620L, ISBN: 978-0689716577*
- *Amelia Earhart, 950L, ISBN: 978-0689831881*
- *Arthur Ashe, 823L, ISBN: 978-0689873461*
- *Davy Crockett, 620L, ISBN: 978-0020418405*
- *Henry Ford, 650L, ISBN: 978-0020419105*
- *Laura Ingalls Wilder, 860L, ISBN: 978-0689839245*
- *Martha Washington, 600L, ISBN: 978-0020421603*
- *Sacagawea, 720L, ISBN: 978-0689714825*
- *Thurgood Marshall, 840L, ISBN: 978-0689820427*
- *Neil Armstrong, 870L, ISBN: 978-0689809958*

Dare to Dream: Coretta Scott King
Angela Shelf Medearis
890L
ISBN: 978-0141302027

This biography details Coretta Scott King's role in the Civil Rights Movement. Black-and-white images and drawings compliment the biographical account. A great example of a secondhand source, this text is crafted from Coretta Scott King's book about her husband. The text chronicles her experiences as a child, activism as an adult, and milestones in her life. Note: the book ends with some suggested reading titles, but both were out-of-print at time of publication.

Fifty Cents and a Dream: Young Booker T. Washington

Jabvari Asir

740L

ISBN: 978-0316086578

This is a touching picture biography of Washington's life. Readers get a peek at some of the early experiences that shaped his life. The watercolor images throughout are engaging and match the tone of the text well. This text is thought-provoking and encourages critical discussions about multiple other subjects.

Gregor Mendel: The Friar Who Grew Peas

Cheryl Bardoe

1030L

ISBN: 978-0810954755

This text traces the life and experiences of the first geneticist. While he was not famous in his own time, his contributions lived on long after his death. The basis for how we examine plants and animals is derived from much of his work. Readers are introduced to his voracious appetite for learning and knowledge, along with the details of some of his genetic theories.

In Their Own Words: Sitting Bull

Peter Roop

700L

ISBN: 978-0439263221

This text is a part of an excellent series called *In Their Own Words*. The great thing about this series is that it offers a narrative-style account of historical figures, combined with images of firsthand sources from the subject. This one shares drawings, letters, and speeches from Sitting Bull. This is a great choice to teach about firsthand and secondhand sources. Students get to differentiate, right in the same text, between sections that are firsthand contrasted with the portions that are secondhand accounts.

When I Was Your Age: Volumes I and II: Original Stories About Growing Up

Amy Ehrlich

930L

ISBN: 978-0763604073

This 200-page book is an anthology of stories about growing up. Written by a variety of famous writers such as Avi, Laurence Yep, Walter Dean Myers, and Joseph Bruchac, the text is really geared toward your fifth graders. Most of the stories are about 20 pages long and work well as stand-alone essays or can be read for contrast, similar themes, and even as writing exemplars. Always preview these vignettes carefully for content and appropriateness for your students.

When Marian Sang: The True Recital of Marian Anderson, the Voice of the Century
Pam Muñoz Ryan
780L
ISBN: 978-0439269674

This biographical text, illustrated by Brian Selznick (*Frindle*), pairs beautiful imagery with narrative storytelling. Ryan details the challenges that Marian Anderson faced as a singer in the racially charged 1930's. Ryan details the overt racism and discrimination that prevented Anderson from being able to perform in some parts of America because of her ethnicity. Filled with beautiful sepia images, a discography, and timeline, this text offers numerous details and text features to engage readers. The text ends with a wordless painting of Anderson finally singing at the Lincoln Memorial during a historic 1939 concert before an integrated audience of almost 80,000 people.

Stealing Home: The Story of Jackie Robinson
Barry Denenberg
930L
ISBN: 978-0590425605

Filled with black-and-white photographs, this text is engaging and detailed. Readers have multiple opportunities to make inferences and support them with details and ideas from the text. This is an engaging text for most students, particularly your baseball fans.

HISTORICAL EVENTS AND GOVERNMENT

Abraham Lincoln and Frederick Douglass: The Story Behind an American Friendship
Russell Freedman
1110L
ISBN: 978-0547385624

Freedman, the author of *Lincoln: A Photobiography,* introduces readers to the parallel lives of these two men. Readers learn how both men grew up poor, were self-educated, and considered slavery morally wrong. Freedman does not gloss over the racial differences and Lincoln's initial avoidance of the Civil War, despite the consequences it would have for slavery. Well thought-out, rich in details, and thought-provoking, this 128-page text is most appropriate for readers who have built up a stamina for longer texts. Freedman includes his own final notes, a bibliography, and an index.

A History of the People: All the People, 1945–2001
Joy Hakim
940L
ISBN: 978-0195153385

This text explores the political and social transitions of this time period. Students learn about major wars such as the Cold War, Vietnam, and the War on Terror. The text also uses photographs of firsthand documents to explain the Declaration of Independence, the Constitution, and the Bill of Rights. Rich images, sidebars, and multiple text structures are throughout the text. Multiple thematic issues are addressed in terms of equality, segregation, and freedom.

A History of US: The First Americans: Prehistory–1600

Joy Hakim

820L

ISBN: 978-0195153194

This 160-page book is a good choice to examine in sections. The information can easily be read sequentially or in a non-linear fashion, depending on your purpose. The full-color text is engaging and offers a visually stimulating, historical explanation of the first Americans.

If You Were There When They Signed the Constitution

Elizabeth Levy

810L

ISBN: 978-0590451598

Readers examine the events of the Constitutional Convention of 1787. This 80-page text features details about the delegates, constitutional issues, and areas of disagreement. This is a great companion text for American history or government units of study.

Those Rebels, John and Tom

Barbara Kerley

960L

ISBN: 978-0545222686

This text, one of the *Orbis Honor Books* of 2013, is sometimes called a dual biography of John Adams and Thomas Jefferson. What is does, at its best, is tell of how two men cooperated, overcame disparate views, and became known as two of the founding fathers of America. The text uses kid-friendly language (at one point describing Thomas Jefferson as "short and stout") and cartoon-like drawings to craft this historical tale of early politics. Numerous informational text standards can be addressed through this book.

MUMMIES, MONSTERS, AND CREATURES

Beastly Tales

Malcolm Yorke

850L

ISBN: 978-0789429629

Readers explore the accounts of famous creatures such as the Sasquatch and the Loch Ness monster. Multiple text features support the reader's understanding. This text also offers readers a chance to summarize, look for main ideas, and compare and contrast.

Bodies from the Bog

James Deem

1100L

ISBN: 978-0395857847

The author introduces readers to the story of Danish workmen who were digging in a peat bog and discovered a dead body. The body was fully preserved. In the text, readers follow scientists as they examine him and explain who he is and how his body was preserved by the peat bog.

Ice Mummy

Mark Dubowski

510L

ISBN: 978-0679856474

This is a text for your emergent readers. While a lower reading-level text, this is a great book to explore text features, point to textual evidence, and support meaning through text features. Readers will enjoy the full-color images and photographs.

The Loch Ness Monster (Solving Mysteries with Science)

Lori Hile

1050L

ISBN: 978-1410949929

Hile uses the scientific method to determine if the Loch Ness monster ever really existed. Detailing the myths surrounding the Loch Ness monster, Hile takes readers on a scientific exploration where mystery and fiction meet science and discovery. This text includes charts, graphs, suggested web resources, call-out boxes, a glossary, and an index.

Mummies: A Strange Science Book

Sylvia Funston

1070L

ISBN: 978-1894379045

Readers learn what qualifies as a mummy, and how they actually become mummified. Readers learn about famous mummies that have been found in Egypt, as well as lesser-known locations where mummies have been found such as China and England. Colorful illustrations and photographs are found throughout the text as well.

Secrets of the Mummies

Shelley Tanaka

1020L

ISBN: 978-0786804733

This text explains how tomb-robbers and visitors often stole the remains of mummies and used them in different ways. The author explains how mummies are preserved using modern technology. This is a great book to explore and analyze reasons, details, evidence, and relationships between individuals, events, and ideas.

The Encyclopedia of Preserved People: Pickled, Frozen, and Mummified Corpses from Around the World

Natalie Jane Prior

1170L

ISBN: 978-0375822872

This text begins by explaining some of the differences between preserved bodies (mummies) and skeletons. This informational text presents basic facts and information in an engaging manner. Filled with images, illustrations, and full-color photographs, students can draw from multiple features to make meaning. There is a comprehensive index and bibliography included as well.

NATURE

A Drop of Water
Walter Wick
870L
ISBN: 978-0590221979
This scientific book is appropriate for early readers. Students trace the evolution of a snow-flake and drop of water throughout the water cycle. Students learn about evaporation and condensation through close-up photographs and a variety of informative text features. Students can actively practice summarizing and sequential order.

Far From Shore: Chronicles of an Open Ocean Voyage
Sophie Webb
1030L
ISBN: 978-0618597291
Readers travel with a young biologist on her adventures. Rich blue pages feature vivid illustrations of dolphins and flying fish, while wonderful text features such as captions, maps, sidebars, diagrams, and charts are found on most pages. This text includes a wide variety of details about the tools and resources that biologists use along with information about the varied creatures that they encounter.

Hurricane and Tornado
Jack Challoner
1090L
ISBN: 978-0756606909
This text outlines the dangers associated with various weather phenomena from around the world. Hail, thunderstorms, lightning, and tornadoes are a few of the weather types that are explored through photographs and text features. This text offers multiple opportunities to compare and contrast, summarize, and draw connections.

Hurricane Katrina Alert!
Ellen Rodger
1120L
ISBN: 978-0778716181
Readers rely on text and photographs to make sense of this natural disaster. The causes and effects of this deadly disaster are explored, along with explanations of specific types of damages and recovery efforts. This text works well for summary, main idea, and text structure.

Volcanoes
Seymour Simon
880L
ISBN: 978-0060877170
The deep, rich photographs found here are enough to draw most readers into this text. Spewing lava and erupting mountains fill about half of the pages of this text. Readers will encounter a wide variety of content-specific vocabulary and organizational structures. This text works well to reinforce multiple informational text standards.

Volcanoes and Other Natural Disasters

Harriet Griffey

830L

ISBN: 978-0789429643

This text explores natural disasters across the globe. Readers investigate multiple geographic regions and learn about a wide variety of volcanoes. The colorful images and variety of text structures help engage readers throughout.

Water for Everyone

Sarah Levete

880L

ISBN: 978-1432924225

Readers learn about the scarcity of water and how people across the globe get their water. Major issues such as water-borne diseases, drought, and water supply are explored. This 32-page text is a great resource to explore summarizing and a wide variety of standards.

Main Idea

"Details create the big picture."
Sanford Weill, *philanthropist*

READING INFORMATIONAL TEXT STANDARD 2:
MAIN IDEA

Third	Fourth	Fifth
Determine the main idea of a text; recount the key details and explain how they support the main idea.	Determine the main idea of a text and explain how it is supported by key details; summarize the text.	Determine two or more main ideas of a text and explain how they are supported by key details; summarize the text.

GRADE LEVEL DIFFERENCES

Each grade level is expected to determine the main idea and key details, then explain how they support one another. In fifth grade this task is expanded to include multiple main ideas. Note that students in third through fifth grade are the last group of students that will use the language of *main idea* for this standard. When students enter sixth grade the appropriate term will be *central idea* instead of *main idea*. This might be a good synonym to begin introducing to your fifth graders.

36

Third Grade

The *Main Idea* standard increases in rigor from third to fifth grade. Third graders have two main goals:

- Determine the focus of the text (main idea).

- Explain how specific details help explain the main idea.

When these third graders progress to the fourth and fifth grade, they will expand their focus to include **summarization**. Let's take a moment to think about the differences here. In the third grade, students look for the main idea and the details. Then, students explain how those details support the main idea. In the fourth and fifth grades students also summarize.

What is a summary? Doesn't a summary explain the main points in the text and include some relevant details? If the standard required third graders to identify or list details, that would be different. The language of the Main Idea standard asks third graders to explain how these details support the main idea. When you add that component in, they have now increased the rigor and the depth of knowledge required to complete this task. The components that the third graders are tasked with explaining *are* the basis of a summary. What does that mean for your instruction? The difference is that a third-grade teacher might not require a written paragraph that carries the label of summary, but students are to receive explicit instruction in the crafting of what will be known as a summary 365 days later.

Fourth Grade

Each of the goals and objectives established in the third grade remain consistent for fourth graders as well. During this school year, students will now be required to craft a summary. In one sense, the standard demands that students look carefully at the underlying ideas of a text. Students need to identify the main idea, write about how it is developed through details, and then summarize what they have read. For fourth-grade students to arrive at mastery, they need to be able to:

- Summarize the text.

- Identify a main idea.

- Understand how details help explain the main idea.

Fifth Grade

These same goals remain consistent as students progress to the fifth grade. The only difference? Fifth graders are asked to look for *two or more main ideas in one text*. What does this mean for instruction? This means that the text choices for your fifth graders need to be intentional. You need to provide practice text and models that have multiple main ideas.

In the fifth grade, introduce the concept that informational text can explore more than one idea simultaneously. Students should be able to identify that there can be **multiple main ideas** in a text. The focus for informational text is to ensure that students can analyze myriad forms of writing. Students should examine magazine articles, blog posts, website content, editorials, and historical documents. Students are analyzing what the author wants them to know and how the author worked to show this through details.

Common Core
Buzzword

Notice that fifth graders are tasked with looking for main ideas. The emphasis is to show that multiple main ideas can exist in one text. Consider your personal reading. How often is a text really just about one main idea? Rarely.

1 **Make a connection between what students have already learned about Standard One: Textual Evidence to the learning for the Main Idea standard.** *"Remember how we looked at photographs and made some judgments about the people in the pictures? We had to rely on evidence to support our thinking. Today we will consider another question. What is this **mostly** about?"*

2 **When you watch television, look at an image, or read a book, there is always a main idea.** *"I want to share the five main idea questions that can help you make some decisions about what the main idea or ideas are."* Create and share the Main Idea Questions anchor chart.

3 **Set the task for the lesson.** *"Today, we are going to watch a few commercials. These commercials have lots of kids, just like you, in them. These kids are going to say lots of different things. While these things may be interesting, the commercial has a* <u>main idea</u> *that the company wants us to learn about. All of the things that the kids say are* <u>details</u> *to help support that main idea. We are going to watch these commercials and think about our five main idea questions. What do you think is the point? After we watch, I will ask you to share what you think is the main idea and what details were used."*

4 **Select 4-5 themed commercials for your students to watch.** I suggest visiting the AT&T YouTube page and selecting the *It's Not Complicated* playlist. (You can find this by searching directly for the AT&T channel on YouTube.) These are great because they have lots of irrelevant details that lead to great discussions about what counts as a **main idea** and what counts as a **detail**. Preview these commercials to make sure that the selected ones have the same message. In most cases, the message is displayed at the end of the commercial as a tag line.

5 **After each commercial, discuss what students see as** *details* **and what they see as the** *main idea.* I like to lead students to the idea that all of the commercials have the same main idea, but use different details to engage viewers and tell entirely different stories. *"Boys and girls, this is exactly what books do! They use lots of different types of details to help you understand or learn about a main idea."* Be certain to point out to your fifth graders that text can and will have more than one main idea.

Standard Two:
{Main Idea Questions}

1. What is the point of this?
2. What does the author want me to learn?
3. What is this really about?
4. What is the message?
5. What BIG idea is here?

Main Idea Questions anchor chart.

6 **Summarize and review the anchor chart with students.** Remind students that they will use these questions whenever they read text to think about the main ideas and details.

38

1 **Select an informational text paragraph or excerpt of text.** I like to use social studies books, newspaper articles, or current events articles from local newspapers, online news sources, or larger national news sources like the *New York Times*. Make sure that students have a copy of the informational text to read along with you.

2 **As you read the text out loud, underline each sentence.** Ask students to think with you about whether that sentence has the BIG idea (or is the main focus of the text) or if it is a detail to help the reader understand the main idea. Talk with students about why you think specific ideas are important. In a sense, you are dissecting the text.

3 **Create a sentence frame and complete it with students to show the main idea and the details.** I like for students to write their ideas and details on large sticky notes and place them on the chart. This let's us be able to move pieces around and work collaboratively.

4 **Repeat this activity as often as necessary.** This will be effective with many different types of informational text.

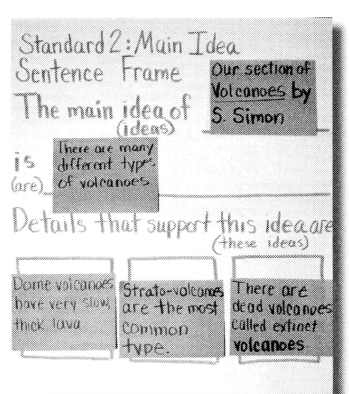

Main Idea Sentence Frame.

THE ORGANIZERS

After you have explicitly introduced and modeled how to apply the strategies of this standard to text, you want to provide students with an organizer that they can use to think about their own informational text reading. In order to make sure that students can independently understand and use the organizer, it is important to model how the specific organizer is used. Select a text and organizer of your choice. Complete the organizer with your students and post it as a model. Afterwards, students can independently use that same organizer multiple times to practice the skill with different informational texts. This can be done in pairs, groups, and independently.

The book that I use with each organizer in this chapter is *Volcanoes* by Seymour Simon. This book is used for each example for this standard for consistency and to offer the same book as a point of comparison for teachers.

1 Read (or reread) *Volcanoes* to your students. If you don't have a copy for each student, project the text or use a document camera so that students can follow along and read it. As you talk with your students, be sure to use the language of this standard. Think out loud and complete the organizer together.

2 Once you model by explicitly completing the organizer, your students will understand the connection between the standard and the organizer. You can provide blank copies of the organizer and allow students to select their own informational text, assign one from your class anthology, or select a title from the suggested book list within this chapter.

3 Students can complete an organizer when they read any informational text. This can be done as an assignment and can be repeated as many times as you want with any informational text that you choose. The sky is the limit! This allows for multiple opportunities to tailor the text to the student and maintain fidelity to the standard.

4 Once students have demonstrated mastery of the skill, don't stop using it. You want your readers to keep practicing. In the introduction of the book, I discussed the pitfalls of being a Checklist Teacher. Students need to keep perfecting their skill sets.

5 Reuse the same organizer, make it into an anchor chart, or post exemplars for students to reference later. You can add the organizer to a standards-based center, pair it with your school's reading incentive program, or use it daily as evidence of reading.

DEVELOPING IDEAS

Stop to discuss any vocabulary that may be challenging or contains an element (like prefixes) that you want to reinforce.

Only your fifth graders will work with two main ideas.

Developing Ideas

Main Ideas

> Ideas about volcanoes have changed over time.

> Volcanoes are both destructive + beneficial.

What details did the author include to support these ideas?

...in the beginning?	...in the middle?	...in the end?
Early people made up stories to explain volcanoes + why we had them	Scientists learned how they were made + that there were different types	After an eruption, life does <u>renew</u> itself. Animals + wildlife return.

How did these details help explain the main ideas?

<u>You see how the</u> early ideas about volcanoes were created.

<u>You get to see</u> how different the facts + ideas are from the <u>myths</u>.

<u>You can see</u> that new landforms and life comes from an eruption.

Writing Connection

After completing this, students have all of the elements for a basic analysis of the text. This can be a summary or the bones of a longer written assignment about a text.

Developing Ideas

Main Ideas

What details did the author include to support these ideas?

...in the beginning?

...in the middle?

...in the end?

How did these details help explain the main ideas?

42

MAIN IDEA WEB

Students have five clear ideas that work well to summarize the text.

Writing Connection

For this activity I start the summary with students and have them continue it on paper. Later, we read our summaries out loud and talk about the summary from a writer's perspective.

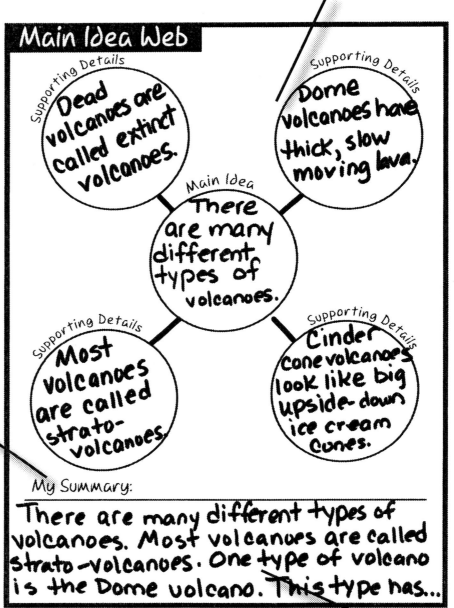

Main Idea Web

Supporting Details
Dead volcanoes are called extinct volcanoes.

Supporting Details
Dome volcanoes have thick, slow moving lava.

Main Idea
There are many different types of volcanoes.

Supporting Details
Most volcanoes are called strato-volcanoes.

Supporting Details
Cinder cone volcanoes look like big upside-down ice cream cones.

My Summary:

There are many different types of volcanoes. Most volcanoes are called strato-volcanoes. One type of volcano is the Dome volcano. This type has...

This is a great time to show the value of transitional words and phrases. "First," "Next," "One way..." easily link ideas here. Students will "get" why they are needed when they see how disjointed their paragraph will be without them.

Main Idea Web

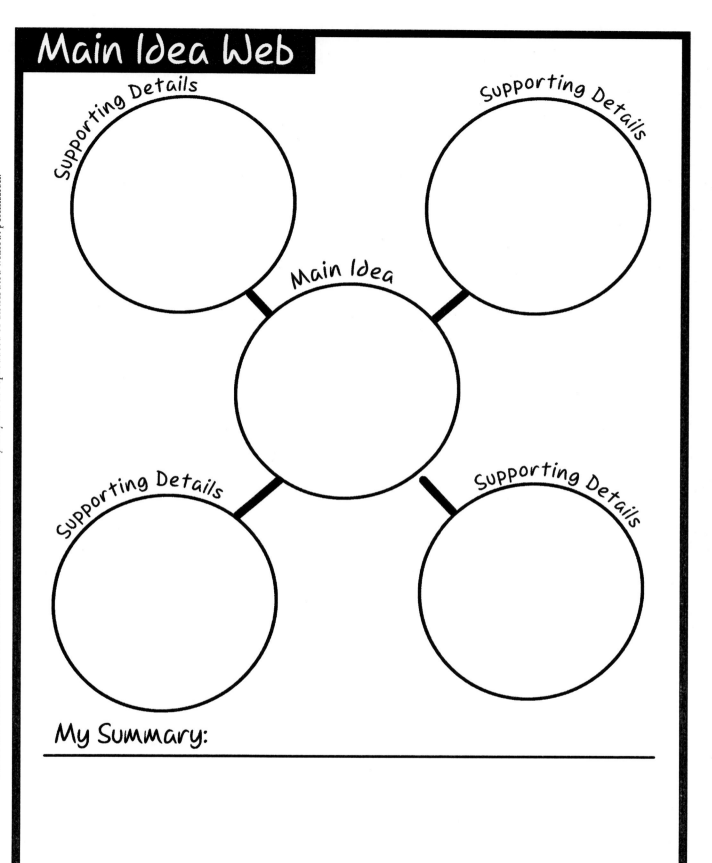

Supporting Details

Supporting Details

Main Idea

Supporting Details

Supporting Details

My Summary:

Two Main Ideas

This organizer is specifically for fifth graders who need to work with two main ideas.

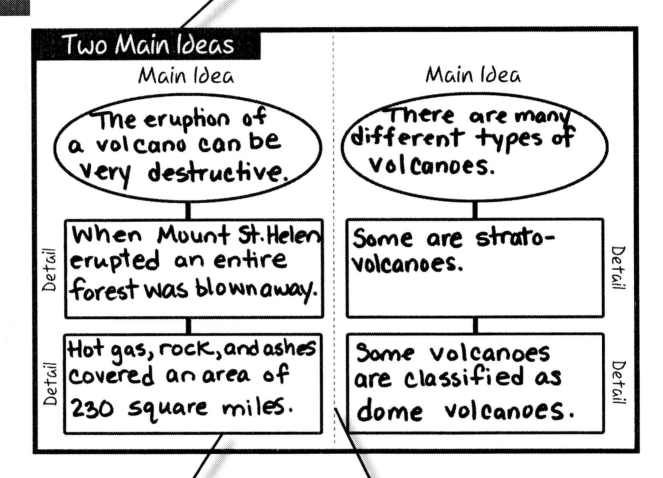

Two Main Ideas

Main Idea

The eruption of a volcano can be very destructive.

Detail

When Mount St. Helen erupted an entire forest was blown away.

Detail

Hot gas, rock, and ashes covered an area of 230 square miles.

Main Idea

There are many different types of volcanoes.

Detail

Some are strato-volcanoes.

Detail

Some volcanoes are classified as dome volcanoes.

Gradual release is the key here! A good idea for this is to have students work in pairs to develop the detail list.

You can cut this in half and place multiple copies in centers. Students can grab one and deconstruct the ideas in any informational text easily.

Two Main Ideas

Main Idea

Detail

Detail

Main Idea

Detail

Detail

EXPLAINING THE DETAILS

Be careful not to focus on students having the same main idea choices. The understanding of details and how they support larger ideas is the focus.

Notice that there can be a wide variety of responses to this question.

This is one of my favorite graphic organizers to enlarge and refer to later. It does a good job of visually tracing the thought process.

Explaining the Details

Main Idea

There are many different stories about how volcanoes are created.

Detail #1

Early Romans believed that Vulcan, the god of fire caused volcanoes.

Detail #2

Early Hawaiians thought Pele, a goddess, caused volcanoes.

?

How does this help me understand the main idea?

- It gives an example.
- It explains one story about Volcanoes
- You also see the similarities between how two different cultures explained volcanoes

?

How does this help me understand the main idea?

- This is an example, too.
- This explains a story and gives details.

Main Idea

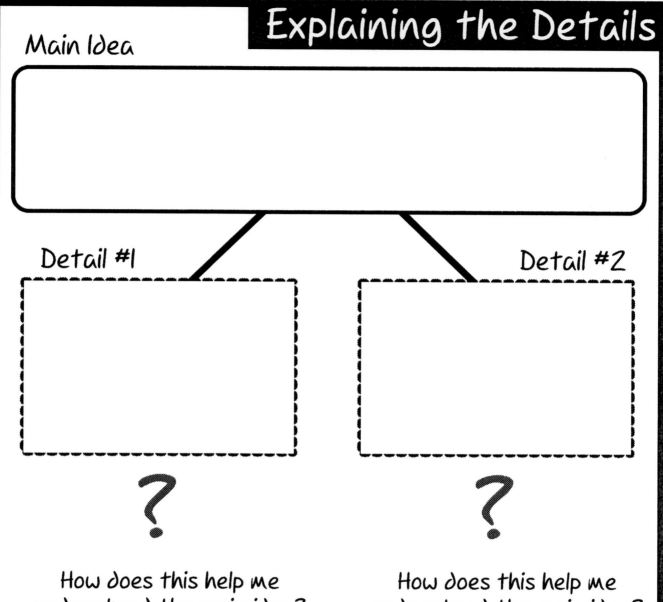

Detail #1

Detail #2

?

?

How does this help me
understand the main idea?

How does this help me
understand the main idea?

This is a great time to refer to the Main Idea Questions anchor chart.

Notice that if the main ideas are inferred, rather than explicit, students can draw on the exact same skill set used for the Textual Evidence standard. This interconnectedness exists across many standards.

2 Details

What did the author try to *explain*?
(Main Idea)

There are many (untrue) stories about what causes a volcano to erupt.

Detail #1

In Hawaii, people used to believe that an angry goddess, Pele, caused volcanic eruptions.

How does this *support* the main idea?

This shows an (example) of a story used to try to explain volcanoes.

Detail #2

Early Romans believed in stories about Vulcan, the God of fire causing volcano eruptions.

How does this *support* the main idea?

This shows that more than one story about the (cause) of volcano eruptions exists.

I like for students to identify HOW specific details support main ideas. This will be helpful when they write and support their own main ideas.

2 Details

What did the author
try to *explain?*
(Main Idea)

Detail #1

How does this support
the main idea?

Detail #2

How does this support
the main idea?

THREE DETAILS

This is the same organizer as "Two Details." This works best with longer text.

3 Details

What did the author try to *explain*? (Main Idea)

There are many (untrue) stories about why volcanoes erupt.

Detail #1	Detail #2	Detail #3
Early Hawaiians told stories of an angry goddess that caused the volcanoes	Early Romans made up stories about a God of Fire causing the volcanoes.	Early scientists didn't have information about why volcanoes happened.

How does this *support* the main idea?

This gives an example/evidence that there were stories.

How does this *support* the main idea?

This gives an example or evidence of a story.

How does this *support* the main idea?

This helps you understand why they made up the stories.

The small boxes really force students to write succinctly and find the core of the idea.

I really try to focus a lot of my discussion on "How." Students need to be able to consider how details are constructed to provide support.

50

3 Details

What did the author
try to explain?
(Main Idea)

Detail #1

How does this support
the main idea?

Detail #2

How does this support
the main idea?

Detail #3

How does this support
the main idea?

American History and Government

A History of the US: Making Thirteen Colonies, 1600–1740
Joy Hakim
860L
ISBN: 978-0195327168
Hakim uses the same vivid and information-packed style that she has become known for in this 192-page text. Each page features various text features, full-color photographs, and rich details and information about the colonies. This is a great text to explore in sections rather than as a cover-to-cover reading assignment.

A History of US: The First Americans: Prehistory–1600
Joy Hakim
820L
ISBN: 978-0195153194
This 160-page book is a good choice to examine in sections. The information can easily be read sequentially or in a non-linear fashion, depending on your purpose. The full-color text is engaging and offers a visually stimulating, historical explanation of the first Americans.

If You Were There When They Signed the Constitution
Elizabeth Levy
810L
ISBN: 978-0590451598
Readers examine the events of the Constitutional Convention of 1787. This 80-page text features details about the delegates, constitutional issues, and areas of disagreement. This is a great companion text for American history or government units of study.

You Wouldn't Want to Sail on the Mayflower!
Peter Cook
960L
ISBN: 978-0531123911
This text is a great complement to many states' social studies curriculum objectives in grades 3-5. Readers will be engaged by the fun illustrations and varied text structures. This is a great text to use when examining organizational patterns and looking at connections between ideas, events, and individuals.

You Wouldn't Want to Sail with Christopher Columbus! ·
Fiona MacDonald
850L
ISBN: 978-0531160602
This text examines some of the hardships and challenges of exploration in this era. Complete with a glossary and an index, this text is formatted like a chapter book, but looks and feels like a picture book. Readers can explore text structure, organizational patterns, and main ideas through this text.

ANIMALS

Animals Nobody Loves
Seymour Simon
860L
ISBN: 978-1587171550
This engaging text pairs vivid images and photographs with interesting and informative facts about 20 different animals. This text works well when teaching students to summarize and identify main ideas and details.

Big Cats
Seymour Simon
1050L
ISBN: 978-0064461191
This award-winning book (*Outstanding Science Trade Books for Children Award*) is all about the different types of cats of the animal kingdom. The text has vivid photographs of jaguars, cheetahs, lions, and pumas. The animal lover in your class will be drawn to this text, as it details how these animals hunt, raise their young, and make their homes. It offers numerous opportunities to examine images and other physical text features for details.

Dogs
Seymour Simon
870L
ISBN: 978-0064462556
This book is a hit with younger children because it explores an animal that most are fond of. Simple and straightforward, Simon's text is written for a pretty young audience. The words are easy to decode and images help explain the text. There are detailed descriptions featured throughout the book. The photographs are touching and vivid, including several two-page spreads. Simon describes the birth and growth of animals, with numerous images of puppies and dogs of different breeds. This is a great introduction to informational text for students who are used to fiction. It is nonthreatening and offers a fun, easily accessible entry point for young readers.

Dolphin Adventure: A True Story

Wayne Grover and Jim Fowler

930L

ISBN: 978-0380732524

This is a firsthand account of Grover's experience with a dolphin family off the coast of Florida. Grover chronicles how he first encountered the dolphin family. He also explains how he came to perform underwater surgery with his diving knife, saving one of the dolphins from dying. Later, one of the dolphins saves Grover from two sharks. Grover does a great job of explaining his feelings and documenting the experience. This is a great text to consider when sharing an example of a firsthand text.

Extreme Animals

Nicola Davies

1100L

ISBN: 978-0763641276

Davies uses vivid colors and varied text features to introduce readers to a wide variety of animals. Focusing on animals that survive in extreme climates, the text explores both habitat and survival techniques of numerous animals. Readers travel underwater, into volcanoes, and to the desert. This text is highly interesting and engaging for young readers.

Outside and Inside Snakes

Sandra Markle

830L

ISBN: 978-0780783348

This informational text provides a great deal of facts, descriptions and details about snakes. The text has a strong focus on snake anatomy, hunting and feeding techniques and how venom works. Detailed descriptions of the snakes' digestive and respiratory systems rely on content-specific words. The text is also effective at crafting comparison and contrast opportunities between humans and snakes. The vivid images, diagrams, and captions offer opportunities to examine the physical text structure as well.

Talented Animals: A Chapter Book

Mary Packard

630L

ISBN: 978-0516244617

This book is a great choice for third graders. The book details the experiences of different animals with unique talents. These include a wide variety of creatures, such as Tillie, a dog who paints, and Koko, the gorilla who uses sign language. This book is filled with colorful photographs, captions, an index, and a wide variety of physical text structures.

Ten True Animal Rescues

Jeanne Betancourt

730L

ISBN: 978-0590681179

This text presents readers with ten different stories where animals rescued or cared for humans. The language is narrative and organized like a chapter book, with chapter lengths ranging from four to ten pages. These survival stories examine a gorilla caring for a young boy and a dolphin that saves the life of a woman. Readers will be engaged and interested in these heart-warming tales.

BIOGRAPHY/ AUTOBIOGRAPHY/ MEMOIR

Childhood of Famous Americans Series
This series of books features the early years of a wide variety of famous Americans. The books do include some fictionalized details, but are engaging choices for young readers. I find that this series works best with third and fourth graders. These books work particularly well when teaching students to look for main ideas and connections across events, ideas, and people. Listed below are some of the more popular biographies published through this series, along with the ISBN and Lexile level. These books work particularly well with the Textual Evidence, Main Idea, and Events and Concepts standards.

- *Abigail Adams, 620L, ISBN: 978-0689716577*
- *Amelia Earhart, 950L, ISBN: 978-0689831881*
- *Arthur Ashe, 823L, ISBN: 978-0689873461*
- *Davy Crockett, 620L, ISBN: 978-0020418405*
- *Henry Ford, 650L, ISBN: 978-0020419105*
- *Laura Ingalls Wilder, 860L, ISBN: 978-0689839245*
- *Martha Washington, 600L, ISBN: 978-0020421603*
- *Sacagawea, 720L, ISBN: 978-0689714825*
- *Thurgood Marshall, 840L, ISBN: 978-0689820427*
- *Neil Armstrong, 870L, ISBN: 978-0689809958*

Father Abraham: Lincoln and His Sons
Harold Holzer
1060L
ISBN: 978-1590783030
This 232-page chapter book is most appropriate for your advanced readers who have built up stamina for longer independent reading. Fifth graders will enjoy reading a less common narrative of Lincoln. This text, organized into fifteen chapters, examines Lincoln's relationships with his four sons. Black-and-white images of Lincoln, his sons, and places that the Lincolns lived are found throughout the text. Readers have multiple opportunities to think critically about relationships, events, and ideas in this text.

Fighting for Equal Rights
Maryann N. Weidt
810L
ISBN: 978-1575051819
This text explores the life of Susan B. Anthony. The text discusses ideas of women's rights, abolition, and equality. It also features the diverse career choices of Anthony, as an activist, journalist, and educator. There are multiple opportunities for connections between ideas, events, and people.

Helen Keller

Leslie Garrett

890L

ISBN: 978-0756603397

This inspirational and factual 128-page text frames Keller as a crusader. Young readers enjoy the plethora of color photographs and the images of various artifacts throughout this text. There are sidebars, definitions, call-out boxes, and multiple text structures that help students make meaning of the events in Keller's life.

Stealing Home: The Story of Jackie Robinson

Barry Denenberg

930L

ISBN: 978-0590425605

Filled with black-and-white photographs, this text is engaging and detailed. Readers have multiple opportunities to make inferences and support them with details and ideas from the text. This is an engaging text for most students, particularly your baseball fans.

We Are the Ship

Kadir Nelson

900L

ISBN: 978-0786808328

This text contains biographical elements, but really tells the story of the Negro Baseball League. Biographical vignettes of players are woven throughout, but the narrative structure really weaves a tale of determination, history, and sacrifice. Vivid colors and engaging descriptions are found throughout the book. This text offers multiple opportunities to ask questions and think critically about individuals, ideas, and events.

INVENTIONS/ INVENTORS

Girls Think of Everything: Stories of Ingenious Inventions by Women

Catherine Thimmesh

960L

ISBN: 978-0618195633

I find that this collection of female biographies is most appropriate for fifth graders. The text includes a good mix of well-known and lesser-known products and women. The biographies are motivating and detailed, featuring many females who became inventors at very young ages. The book, sprinkled with pops of pink text, includes an expansive timeline, images, and call-out boxes with different quotes and facts. This book can be used to model and reinforce multiple standards.

High-Tech Inventions: A Chapter Book

Mary Packard

770L

ISBN: 978-0516246840

This is a collection of short stories about technological inventions. This short chapter book explores inventions that are as varied as the first computer to a remote-controlled cockroach. Readers will enjoy the captions, photos, and sidebars.

Mistakes That Worked: 40 Familiar Inventions and How They Came to Be
Charlotte Foltz Jones
1040L
ISBN: 978-0385320436

Jones, a magazine writer by trade, brings her knowledge of informational writing to this text. Written with a level of text complexity that will challenge students, the text is still extremely accessible. Some of the inventions include Popsicles, the piggy bank, doughnut holes, and Coca-Cola. Jones does a great job of introducing fun inventions with expansive details. Featuring a reference page, an index, illustrations, and a table of contents, this 96-page book is a great source to study text structure, main idea, and virtually any of the other informational text standards.

Mr. Blue Jeans: A Story About Levi Strauss
Maryann N. Weidt
960L
ISBN: 978-0876145883

Readers are introduced to the man behind the Levi Jeans company. The text details the humble beginnings of his life as a Jewish immigrant. Readers make sense of the text through multiple text features including captions, an index, bibliography, maps, and images. This is an appropriate text to reinforce multiple standards.

Toys! Amazing Stories Behind Some Great Inventions
Don Wulffson
920L
ISBN: 978-0805061963

This text is such an engaging collection of short informational text essays. Organized to read like short articles, each section of this book explains the origin of a different type of toy. Over 25 different toys are featured here, including Mr. Potato Head, Raggedy Ann, Twister, Silly Putty, and Trivial Pursuit. Students will devour the content and stay engaged with the text.

PLACES

Afghanistan
Ann Heinrichs
710L
ISBN: 978-0516227757

This 48-page text examines the culture, physical features, and resources of Afghanistan. Readers have sidebars, a glossary, an index, and numerous text features to help them make meaning. There is also a recommended reading list for students to learn more.

Ancient Greece
Sandra Newman
850L
ISBN: 978-0531252260
Through colorful images, varied and brightly-colored text, readers learn about the Olympics, science, art, and government of ancient Greece. Organized into six chapters, this text does a good job of showing the accomplishments commonly associated with Greece and the relationship to today's culture and government. Captions, sidebars, photographs, and a glossary are just a few of the text structures that students will encounter.

Australia
Sean McCollum
760L
ISBN: 978-0822571261
Through chapter titles like "Aussie Talk," "Critters," and "What to Read," students learn about the art, history, sports, and food of Australia. Vivid colors fill almost every page of this text, with vibrant and varied text structures throughout. This 48-page text is an engaging and informative voyage into the history and culture of Australia.

Looking at Germany
Kathleen Pohl
730L
ISBN: 978-0836887679
This 32-page book provides a wide variety of facts and details about Germany. Students are able to learn about the country's features, people, food, and weather. Maps, images, and photographs help readers make meaning from the text.

WEATHER

Blizzard! The Storm That Changed America
Jim Murphy
1080L
ISBN: 978-0590673105
Murphy uses a wide variety of firsthand documents to explain the infamous snowstorm of 1888. Organized into eight chapters with titles like "The Unholy One" and "Just a Baby," this text includes a wide variety of sentence lengths and structures to explain events. Newspaper articles and personal stories are also presented to paint a comprehensive picture.

Can it Rain Cats and Dogs? Questions and Answers About Weather
Melvin Berger
710L
ISBN: 978-0439085731
Organized to provide answers to a series of questions about weather, this text is accessible for all readers. Bright colors and vivid photographs are found on virtually every page. The

simple, but factual, writing style makes this a straightforward text. This is a great text to practice summarizing and to examine connections.

Getting to the Bottom of Global Warming
Terry Collins
780L
ISBN: 978-1429639729

This text is presented in a graphic-novel format. Readers follow the experiences of Isabel Soto. Soto learns about global warming and takes the reader along. The text explains numerous aspects of global warming in a clear, easy-to-understand format. At just 32 pages, this text presents a great deal of information.

Hurricane and Tornado
Jack Challoner
1090L
ISBN: 978-0756606909

This text outlines the dangers associated with various weather phenomena from around the world. Hail, thunderstorms, lightning, and tornadoes are a few of the weather types that are explored through photographs and text features. This text offers multiple opportunities to compare and contrast, summarize, and draw connections.

Severe Storm and Blizzard Alert
Lynn Peppas
1050L
ISBN: 978-0778716051

Readers examine the impact of hail, wind, storms, and lightning in this 32-page book. Readers are exposed to content-specific vocabulary throughout this science text. Practical explanations of Doppler radar are balanced with more dramatic descriptions of the Blizzard of 1888.

Tornado: Nature in Action
Stephen Kramer
940L
ISBN: 978-1575050584

This text examines the dangers of a tornado. Up-close photographs of the devastation and aftermath of tornadoes are included throughout the text. Readers learn what happens inside of storm clouds and practical ways to stay safe. Readers can identify main ideas and connections with this book. The wealth of maps, charts, graphs, and tables make this an appropriate choice for text structure.

Events & Concepts

"A book is not an isolated being; it is a relationship, an axis of innumerable relationships."
Jorge Luis Borges, *author*

READING INFORMATIONAL TEXT STANDARD 3:
EVENTS & CONCEPTS

Third	Fourth	Fifth
Describe the relationship between a series of historical events, scientific ideas or concepts, or steps in technical procedures in a text, using language that pertains to time, sequence, and cause/effect.	Explain events, procedures, ideas, or concepts in a historical, scientific, or technical text, including what happened and why, based on specific information in the text.	Explain the relationships or interactions between two or more individuals, events, ideas, or concepts in a historical, scientific, or technical text based on specific information in the text.

GRADE LEVEL DIFFERENCES

Each grade level looks for events, ideas, and concepts within historical, scientific, and technical text. Third and fourth graders also examine steps/procedures, while fifth graders add individuals as the fourth area of analysis. Once you move beyond text type, the standard varies across the grade levels. This is one of the standards where third and fifth graders have congruent tasks, but the fourth-grade goal is the outlier. Fourth graders just need to explain what happened and why. Third and fifth graders both examine the specific interactions and relationships between each concept.

The *Events and Concepts* standard varies quite a bit across each grade level. Let's begin by looking at the similarities for the three grade levels. There is a focus on three specific types of informational text: **historical, scientific,** and **technical.** Each grade level is tasked with explaining events, ideas, and concepts. Events are often historical; examples could include a presidential election or a war. Concepts, by definition, are abstract ideas or general notions. For example: the concept of multiplication or the concept of gravity. An example of an idea could be that *pay should be linked to performance* or the idea that *the world is flat.* Ideas are often mental impressions; this line of distinction is so slight and gray that I always suggest that teachers consider these as one category. Distinctions can be made, but they are often subjective and minimal in terms of the core learning of this standard. This leaves students with two consistent types of information to consider in a text: (1) events, and (2) ideas/concepts.

Let's examine the critical differences for each grade level. Third and fifth grade are more congruent and fourth grade is the outlier.

Fourth Grade

Fourth graders explain events, ideas/concepts, and procedures. Students are simply to explain what happened and why it happened. The language of the standard never refers to the examination of specific relationships between these three. In the previous and the following grade levels, however, students have to explain and make connections across these categories.

Third and Fifth Grade

In the third and fifth grade, students focus on the relationships between three different categories of information. Third graders are considering events, ideas/concepts, and *steps.* Fifth graders focus on events, ideas/concepts, and *individuals.* You will note that in the third-grade standard it specifically says that students should use language that pertains to time, sequence, and cause/effect. Many people see

that language and assume that they are teaching patterns of organization or text structure. This is a misconception. When you examine text structure, you are looking at organization. For this standard you are looking at the specific content *within* those three categories. Don't accidently replace the goals of this standard with Text Structure (Standard Five) or Evidence and Connections (Standard Eight). Your students are focusing on events, ideas/concepts, and steps (third grade) or individuals (fifth grade) as they look for relationships.

So what exactly is a *relationship?* A simple way to think about this is to consider that students are identifying links between the three categories. *What does one category have to do with the other?* Students are thinking about these relationships. This demands the close reading of a text and the ability to make some judgment calls. Connections made by students will be diverse and varied. The focus is not on students identifying the *same* relationship; the goal is to help students consider how *at least two* of these categories *interact.* In the third grade, the language of the standard is really only about two types of relationships: cause/effect and time sequence.

For fifth graders, the standard does not specifically list the types of relationships required for the standard. The goal here is to focus on multiple types of relationships and encourage students to negotiate which types of relationships they note. These relationships typically come in one of the following forms (but are definitely not limited to these):

► **Cause/Effect**
► **Problem/Solution**
► **Compare/Contrast**
► **Time Sequence**

When fifth graders work on Text Structure (Standard Five), they will begin to look at how entire sections of text are organized in these same ways. For the Events & Concepts standard, students are simply tasked with pulling out events, individuals, concepts, steps, or ideas and looking for interactions.

1 **Begin with the idea that there are relationships and connections all around us.** *"Everything is connected or related in some way. You can literally make a connection between almost any two ideas, individuals, or events. This school year, we will look at relationships between people (like you and I), events (like a war, an invention, or a celebration), and ideas (like honesty, fairness, or gravity)."* Elaborate here or consider a mini-lesson on events, ideas, steps, or individuals based on your students' level of understanding of these terms and the grade level that you teach.

2 **Introduce the five types of connections found in informational text.** *"Today I am going to share five types of connections that you will notice a lot when you read informational text."* Create the anchor chart with students, asking them to record their own visual representations of each type of connection/relationship.

3 **Encourage students to think about individuals, ideas, or events from the media, text, school or home that are connected in one of the five ways.** Record student ideas to create a class list on the board. Spend time discussing the relationships.

4 **Review the five connections and explain that students will continue to look for these relationships as they read informational text.** Post the anchor chart so that it remains visible.

RI3: Events & Concepts
Big Event ←influences One Person
Problem ←that needs a→ Solution
Cause ←of a specific Effect
Similarities ←and/or→ Differences
Sequence→ Steps→Order→1-2-3
What relationships do you see ???

The Five Types of Connections Found in 3-5 Informational Text.

1 Ask students to think of individuals, events, ideas, or steps that they have read about or seen on television, or other type of media. Try to get many different responses. I find that it is best to focus on one type of relationship at a time. I like to begin with *One Person/Big Event.* This is often easy to understand, yet powerful. Challenge your students to think of individuals that they have read about who have influenced a larger event. Add these ideas to one anchor chart for future reference.

2 When you have done this, select an informational text to read aloud. As you prepare to think out loud with your students, make sure that each have their own copies or be able to access the text through an overhead projector or an interactive whiteboard.

3 As you read, tell students that you are going to look for:
- Individuals (fifth grade) or Steps (third grade)
- Events
- Ideas/Concepts

4 Assign each category a color sticky note. For example:
- Individuals or Steps (yellow)
- Events (blue)
- Ideas (pink)

5 As you read aloud, stop when you get to an individual/step, idea, or event. Discuss it and record it on the corresponding color sticky note. Stick the notes on the board or in a visible place for all students.

6 After you have read the piece, tell students that you want to see if they can make connections between any of the ideas, events, individuals, or steps. Think out loud as you begin pairing them together, explaining the relationship as you go. I like to let students move the sticky notes around.

One Person 👤	Big Event 🌐
1. Superman	Saves the Earth
2. Abraham Lincoln	End of Slavery
3. Martin Luther King, Jr.	Civil Rights Movement
4. LeBron James	Winning Season
5. George Washington	Revolutionary War

Class anchor chart on One Person/Big Event Connections.

THE ORGANIZERS

After you have explicitly introduced and modeled how to apply the strategies of this standard to text, you want to provide students with an organizer that they can use to think about their own informational text reading. In order to make sure that students can independently understand and use the organizer, it is important to model how the specific organizer is used. Select a text and organizer of your choice. Complete the organizer with your students and post it as a model. Afterwards, students can independently use that same organizer multiple times to practice the skill with different informational texts. This can be done in pairs, groups, and independently.

The book that I use with each organizer in this chapter is *A History of US: The First Americans: Prehistory–1600* by Joy Hakim. This book is used for each example for this standard for consistency and to offer the same book as a point of comparison for teachers.

1 Read (or reread) one to two pages from *A History of US: The First Americans: Prehistory–1600* to your students. For these examples I read from pages 138 and 139. If you don't have a copy for each student, project the text or use a document camera so that students can follow along and read it. As you talk with your students, be sure to use the language of this standard. Think out loud and complete the organizer together.

2 Once you model by explicitly completing the organizer, your students will understand the connection between the standard and the organizer. You can provide blank copies of the organizer and allow students to select their own informational text, assign one from your class anthology, or select a title from the suggested book list within this chapter.

3 Students can complete an organizer when they read any informational text. This can be done as an assignment and can be repeated as many times as you want with any informational text that you choose. The sky is the limit! This allows for multiple opportunities to tailor the text to the student and maintain fidelity to the standard.

4 Once students have demonstrated mastery of the skill, don't stop using it. You want your readers to keep practicing. In the introduction of the book, I discussed the pitfalls of being a Checklist Teacher. Students need to keep perfecting their skill sets.

5 Reuse the same organizer, make it into an anchor chart, or post exemplars for students to reference later. You can add the organizer to a standards-based center, pair it with your school's reading incentive program, or use it daily as evidence of reading.

THREE EVENTS

Extend the
Thinking

This is a favorite among students. They have a lot of flexibility to choose what events they share.

3 Events

What Happened?

> King Henry VIII was very angry with the Pope.

➤

Why?

> He would not grant him a divorce from his wife.

What Happened?

> Many people in England became Anglican.

➤

Why?

> Henry VIII formed the church and called it the "true" church.

What Happened?

> People called Queen Mary "Bloody Mary."

➤

Why?

> She had many people killed to try to make them all Catholic again.

Scaffold this activity by filling in some of the boxes and letting students complete the remainder.

Be certain to point out the direct link to cause-and-effect here.

3 Events

Why?

Why?

Why?

What Happened?

What Happened?

What Happened?

CAUSE & EFFECT

This was modeled using one call-out box from the text (p. 138). This shows students how cause and effect relationships can be found in short or long sections of text.

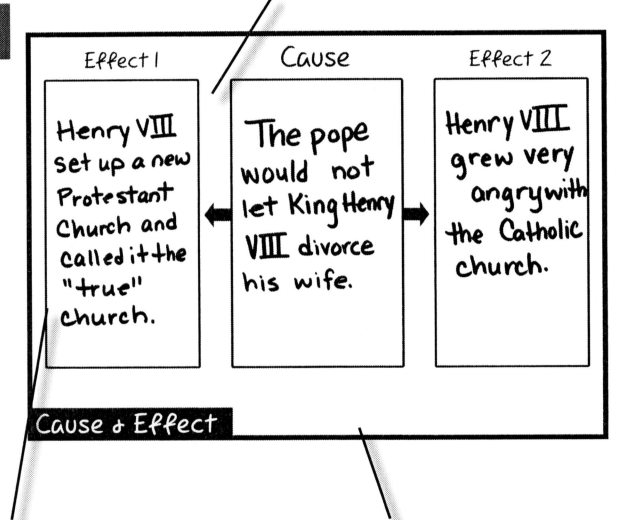

Effect 1

Henry VIII set up a new Protestant Church and called it the "true" church.

Cause

The pope would not let King Henry VIII divorce his wife.

Effect 2

Henry VIII grew very angry with the Catholic church.

Cause & Effect

This graphic organizer allows students to write a lot for each section! They have to think through what they want to share.

A good way to scaffold this for students is to give them either a cause or an effect and let them determine the rest.

Effect 2

Cause

Effect 1

Cause & Effect

COMPARE IDEAS, EVENTS, AND INDIVIDUALS

You may want to begin with the comparison of just two ideas and build up to three.

"Individuals" is only identified in the fifth-grade standard. Third graders look for "steps."

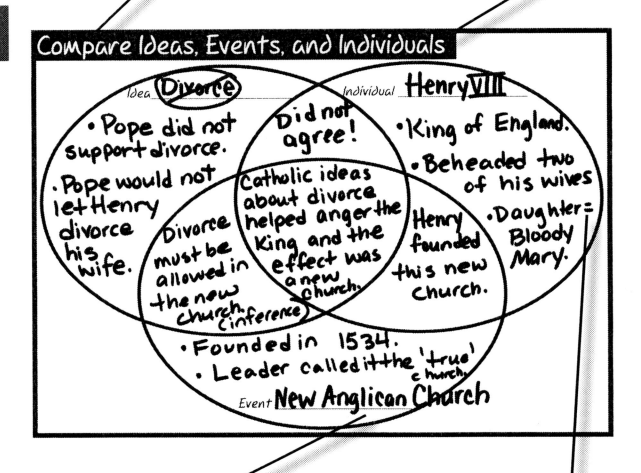

Compare Ideas, Events, and Individuals

Idea **Divorce**

• Pope did not support divorce.
• Pope would not let Henry divorce his wife.

Did not agree!

Divorce must be allowed in the new church (inference)

Catholic ideas about divorce helped anger the King and the effect was a new church.

Individual **Henry VIII**

• King of England.
• Beheaded two of his wives
• Daughter = Bloody Mary.

Henry founded this new church.

• Founded in 1534.
• Leader called it the 'true' church.

Event **New Anglican Church**

An alternative is to give students a partially-completed organizer and let them complete the rest in collaborative pairs or independently.

Space is always a challenge when you compare three things. Symbols and shorthand are usually necessary.

Compare Ideas, Events, and Individuals

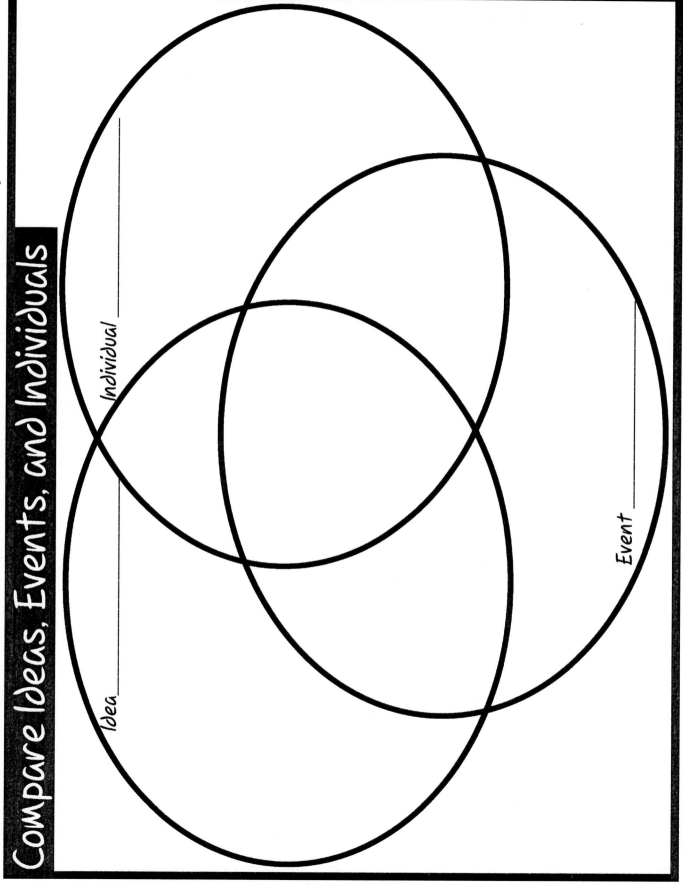

Individual _____

Idea _____

Event _____

CONNECTION?

This is a fun organizer that I like to turn into a game. Whatever idea I connect second has to be used again to make a connection. Note here, Henry VIII was used twice. Then the Anglican Church was used. Kids love to try to think of connections.

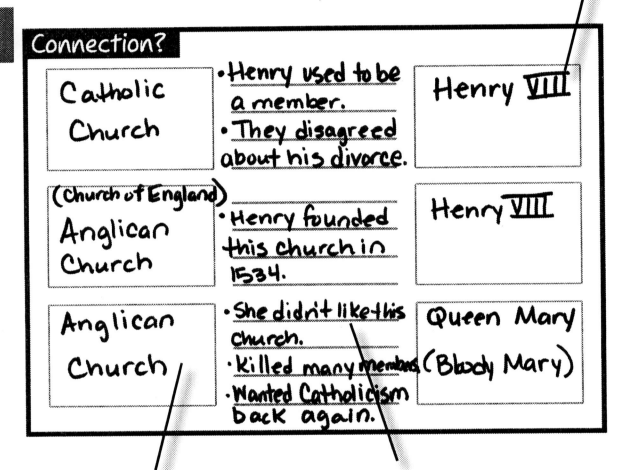

Connection?

Catholic Church	• Henry used to be a member. • They disagreed about his divorce.	Henry VIII
Anglican Church (Church of England)	• Henry founded this church in 1534.	Henry VIII
Anglican Church	• She didn't like this church. • Killed many members • Wanted Catholicism back again.	Queen Mary (Bloody Mary)

This is a great organizer to use to aid in the close reading of a text.

You will be amazed at the variety of responses students come up with for this organizer. They enjoy the flexibility.

Connection?

IF . . . THEN

Explain vocabulary choices as you model this organizer.

Short on copies? This is a fast and easy organizer for students to recreate.

If . . . Then

If . . .
The Pope had granted (given) the King his divorce...

Then:
King Henry VIII might not have started his own church.

If . . .
Queen Mary did not have Protestants Killed for their religion.

Then:
The people might not have nicknamed her "Bloody Mary."

If . . .
King Henry VIII was not the King...

Then:
Not as many people would have followed his lead and left the Catholic Church.

Notice the scratched-out apostrophe. I love to create intentional mistakes in usage to open up a teachable moment and show kids that it is OK to make mistakes.

This organizer is one of the BEST for critical thinking. Students have to make connections and use higher-order thinking.

If . . . . Then

If . . . .

Then:

If . . . .

Then:

If . . . .

Then:

MAPPING OUT RELATIONSHIPS

A way to scaffold initially is to just have students fill in the boxes, but not identify the relationship type until they have had more practice.

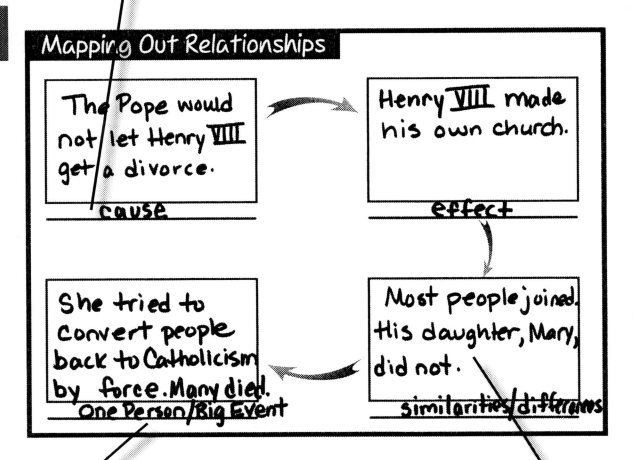

Mapping Out Relationships

The Pope would not let Henry VIII get a divorce.
__cause__

Henry VIII made his own church.
__effect__

She tried to convert people back to Catholicism by force. Many died.
__One Person/Big Event__

Most people joined. His daughter, Mary, did not.
__similarities/differences__

Notice that many of the relationship types can fit. This is appropriate. In real life there are multiple relationships that exist between ideas and events!

This works as a great companion to virtually any social studies content or text.

Mapping Out Relationships

SEQUENCING EVENTS

Point out that sequential ideas are connected with transitional words like these.

This organizer works well when you expect much more detail from your students. They can add details and really elaborate much more here.

Sequencing Events

First . . .

King Henry VIII changed from being a Catholic to his own church. This church became the Church of England.

Then . . .

When his daughter grew up she did not agree or like the new church. She tried to make England a Catholic country again. She had the support of her husband, Phillip.

Finally . . .

Many people in England were killed because of Mary and Phillip's choices. The people named her "Bloody Mary".

Writing Connection

This is also a good time to talk about how to turn this sequence of events into a summary.

Sequencing Events

First . . . .

Then . . . .

Finally . . . .

THINKING ABOUT EVENTS

This organizer combines both Standard 3 and Standard 1. It is always good practice to ask students to explain how they know. Justifying responses is critical to understand their thinking.

Distinguish between explicit (right there) information and implicit information (inferences) by using quotation marks.

Thinking About Events

The text said Mary had them killed and named her Bloody Mary. That means A LOT!

How do you know?

"She never liked the Anglican church."

What Happened?

Why?

Many people died in the 1500s. These people were Protestants.

She did not like the Protestants and thought she could force everyone to be Catholic again.

when I made this, we noticed that "Protestant" should be capitalized because it was a proper noun. we stopped and had a 3-minute discussion about proper nouns and left the corrected error as a reminder.

Thinking About Events

How do
you
know?

Why?

What Happened?

AMERICAN HISTORY

A History of US: Making Thirteen Colonies, 1600–1740
Joy Hakim
860L
ISBN: 978-0195327168

Hakim uses the same vivid and information-packed style that she has become known for in this 192-page text. Each page features various text features, full-color photographs, and rich details and information about the colonies. This is a great text to explore in sections rather than as a cover-to-cover reading assignment.

A History of US: The First Americans: Prehistory–1600
Joy Hakim
820L
ISBN: 978-0195153194

This 160-page book is a good choice to examine in sections. The information can easily be read sequentially or in a non-linear fashion, depending on your purpose. The full-color text is engaging and offers a visually stimulating, historical explanation of the first Americans.

Colonial Life
Brendan January
770L
ISBN: 978-0516271941

January explains about the farming, medicine and food of the colonists. Readers learn about the branches of government and important American symbols. The glossary, word list, and index help readers to navigate the text and understand content-specific words and concepts.

The New Americans: Colonial Times: 1620–1689
Betsy Maestro
940L
ISBN: 978-0060575724

In this 48-page book, readers learn about the different European countries that explored the New World and the resulting colonies. Rich watercolors fill most pages, often covering the whole page, with the text set right inside. Readers will encounter content-specific vocabulary and a wealth of details about colonial life.

Those Rebels, John and Tom
Barbara Kerley
960L
ISBN: 978-0545222686

This text, one of the *Orbis Honor Books* of 2013, is sometimes called a dual biography of

John Adams and Thomas Jefferson. What is does, at its best, is tell of how two men cooperated, overcame disparate views, and became known as two of the founding fathers of America. The text uses kid-friendly language (at one point describing Thomas Jefferson as "short and stout") and cartoon-like drawings to craft this historical tale of early politics. Numerous informational text standards can be addressed through this book.

BIOGRAPHY/ AUTOBIOGRAPHY/ MEMOIR

Buried Alive! How 33 Miners Survived 69 Days Deep Under the Chilean Desert
Elaine Scott
1060L
ISBN: 978-0547707785
This text chronicles the story of the 33 miners that were trapped under the Chilean desert in 2010. Readers learn of the dangers associated with mining. A suggested reading list, glossary, and a wide variety of firsthand stories are included. There are also strong themes of community, problem-solving, and hope. Multiple standards can be supported by this text.

Can You Fly High, Wright Brothers?
Melvin Berger and Gilda Berger
720L
ISBN: 978-0439833783
This text combines interesting facts about the Wright brothers' early lives with a wealth of information about the more well-known events in their lives. Filled with vivid illustrations, photographs, and wonderful text features, this text is engaging for students in all grades.

Childhood of Famous Americans Series
This series of books features the early years of a wide variety of famous Americans. The books do include some fictionalized details, but are engaging choices for young readers. I find that this series works best with third and fourth graders. These books work particularly well when teaching students to look for main ideas and connections across events, ideas, and people. Listed below are some of the more popular biographies published through this series, along with the ISBN and Lexile level. These books work particularly well with the Textual Evidence, Main Idea, and Events and Concepts standards.

- *Abigail Adams, 620L, ISBN: 978-0689716577*
- *Amelia Earhart, 950L, ISBN: 978-0689831881*
- *Arthur Ashe, 823L, ISBN: 978-0689873461*
- *Davy Crockett, 620L, ISBN: 978-0020418405*
- *Henry Ford, 650L, ISBN: 978-0020419105*
- *Laura Ingalls Wilder, 860L, ISBN: 978-0689839245*
- *Martha Washington, 600L, ISBN: 978-0020421603*
- *Sacagawea, 720L, ISBN: 978-0689714825*
- *Thurgood Marshall, 840L, ISBN: 978-0689820427*
- *Neil Armstrong, 870L, ISBN: 978-0689809958*

Dare to Dream: Coretta Scott King
Angela Shelf Medearis
890L
ISBN: 978-0141302027
This biography details Coretta Scott King's role in the Civil Rights Movement. Black-and-white images and drawings compliment the biographical account. A great example of a secondhand source, this text is crafted from Coretta Scott King's book about her husband. The text chronicles her experiences as a child, activism as an adult, and milestones in her life. Note: the book ends with some suggested reading titles, but both were out-of-print at time of publication.

End Zone
Tiki Barber and Ronde Barber
830L
ISBN: 978-1416990970
This heart-warming book is one of my personal favorites to read out loud with my students. Football fans and students with siblings, in particular, will be drawn to this tale of brothers who lead their junior high teammates to a state football championship. Both grow up to be real-life professional football players. The text offers quite a few opportunities to make connections between individuals, ideas, and events.

Gregor Mendel: The Friar Who Grew Peas
Cheryl Bardoe
1030L
ISBN: 978-0810954755
This text traces the life and experiences of the first geneticist. While he was not famous in his own time, his contributions lived on long after his death. The basis for how we examine plants and animals is derived from much of his work. Readers are introduced to his voracious appetite for learning and knowledge, along with the details of some of his genetic theories.

In Their Own Words: Sitting Bull
Peter Roop
700L
ISBN: 978-0439263221
This text is a part of a great series called *In Their Own Words*. The great thing about this series is that it offers a narrative-style account of historical figures, combined with images of firsthand sources from the subject. This one shares drawings, letters, and speeches from Sitting Bull. This is a great choice to teach about firsthand and secondhand sources. Students get to differentiate, right in the same text, between sections that are firsthand contrasted with the portions that are secondhand accounts.

Life in the Ocean: The Story of Oceanographer Sylvia Earle
Claire Nivola
1170L
ISBN: 978-0374380687
Readers are introduced to Sylvia Earle's early life as she grows up on a farm in Paulsboro,

New Jersey. Introspective moments are shared as Earle reflects on her journal writing and early musings. Readers follow Earle as her family moves to Clearwater, Florida and Earle falls in love with the beauty of the Gulf of Mexico. Readers learn of her experiences and the choices that led her to an eventual career as an oceanographer. Inspiring and relatable, this text is a great example of narrative nonfiction.

INVENTIONS/ INVENTORS

Girls Think of Everything: Stories of Ingenious Inventions by Women
Catherine Thimmesh
960L
ISBN: 978-0618195633
I find that this collection of female biographies is most appropriate for fifth graders. The text includes a good mix of well-known and lesser-known products and women. The biographies are motivating and detailed, featuring many females who invented their creations at very young ages. The book, sprinkled with pops of pink text, includes an expansive time-line, images, and call-out boxes with different quotes and facts. This book can be used to model and reinforce multiple standards.

Louis Braille, The Boy Who Invented Books for the Blind
Margaret Davidson
510L
ISBN: 978-0590443500
This biography traces the life of this 19th-century inventor. Readers learn about how the language was invented and the context of the invention. This is an excellent text to support instruction on time sequence, main ideas, and summarizing.

Mistakes That Worked: 40 Familiar Inventions and How They Came to Be
Charlotte Foltz Jones
1040L
ISBN: 978-0385320436
Jones, a magazine writer by trade, brings her knowledge of informational writing to this text. Written with a level of text complexity that will challenge students, the text is still extremely accessible. Some of the inventions include Popsicles, the piggy bank, doughnut holes, and Coca-Cola. Jones does a great job of introducing fun inventions with expansive details. Featuring a reference page, an index, illustrations, and a table of contents, this 96-page book is a great source to study text structure, main idea, and virtually any of the other informational text standards.

The Kid Who Invented the Popsicle: And Other Surprising Stories About Inventions
Don Wulffson
1080L
ISBN: 978-0141302041
This book is my absolute favorite to use for any type of modeling. The short informational text lends itself to both being read out loud or independently. I also enjoy that the topics

are all presented on one page. This allows you to read and discuss an entire invention with your students rather than just an excerpt. Written by Don Wulffson, who is known for his writing on kid-friendly inventions, the text has his trademark fun writing style and quirky introduction to facts and details. The text includes a wide variety of facts that most adults don't know. Fully engaging and just plain fun, this text can be used for multiple standards.

Toys! Amazing Stories Behind Some Great Inventions
Don Wulffson
920L
ISBN: 978-0805061963
This text is such an engaging collection of short informational text essays. Organized to read like short articles, each section of this text explains the origin of a different type of toy. Over 25 different toys are featured in this text, including Mr. Potato Head, Raggedy Ann, Twister, Silly Putty, and Trivial Pursuit. Students will devour the content and stay engaged with the text.

ENVIRONMENT AND WEATHER

Can it Rain Cats and Dogs? Questions and Answers About Weather
Melvin Berger
710L
ISBN: 978-0439085731
Organized to provide answers to a series of questions about weather, this text is accessible for all readers. Bright colors and vivid photographs are found on virtually every page. The simple, but factual, writing style makes this a straightforward text. This is a great text to practice summarizing and to examine connections.

Green Living
Lucia Raatma
900L
ISBN: 978-0756542450
This 64-page text explores the concept of green living. Readers learn about environmental protection in an easy-to-understand format. The author uses content-specific vocabulary to provide an overview of major issues and lifestyle choices associated with environmental protection efforts.

The Most Beautiful Roof in the World: Exploring the Rainforest Canopy
Kathryn Lasky and Christopher G. Knight
1160L
ISBN: 978-0152008970
This 48-page informational text focuses on the rainforest canopy. Students follow biologist Meg Lowman and her assistant as they explore and document the plant and animal life found in the Belize rainforest canopy. The authors explain the specific methods that

scientists use to conduct research and collect specimens and samples from the rainforest. The text also documents Lowman's relationship with her two sons, who have come along on her adventure. This book is definitely geared more towards your fifth graders and can be challenging, despite its relatively short length.

Volcanoes and Other Natural Disasters
Harriet Griffey
830L
ISBN: 9780789429643

This text explores natural disasters across the globe. Readers investigate multiple geographic regions and learn about a wide variety of volcanoes. The colorful images and variety of text structures help engage readers throughout.

Water for Everyone
Sarah Levete
880L
ISBN: 9781432924225

Readers learn about the scarcity of water and how people across the globe get their water. Major issues such as water-borne diseases, drought, and water supply are explored. This 32-page text is a great resource to explore summarizing and a wide variety of standards.

MUMMIES, MONSTERS, AND CREATURES

Beastly Tales
Malcolm Yorke
850L
ISBN: 978-0789429629

Readers explore the accounts of famous creatures such as the Sasquatch and the Loch Ness monster. Multiple text features support the reader's understanding. This text also offers readers a chance to summarize, look for main ideas, and compare and contrast.

Bog Bodies
Natalie Jane Prior
1110L
ISBN: 978-1864482430

This 96-page book explores a wide variety of mummies and human corpses. The images will be sure to excite and delight your readers who enjoy the gross and creepy! The author explains what a bog body is and how it is preserved. Full-color photographs appear throughout the text.

Cat Mummies
Kelly Trumble
870L
ISBN: 978-0395968918
This engaging chapter book shows how Egyptian mummification was not just for humans. The author uses color-washed illustrations to walk readers through the reasons why cats were sacred to Egyptians, how they were mummified, and the thousands of cat mummies that have been found.

Secrets of the Mummies
Shelley Tanaka
1020L
ISBN: 978-0786804733
This text explains how tomb-robbers and visitors often stole the remains of mummies and used them in different ways. The author explains how mummies are preserved using modern technology. This is a great book to explore and analyze reasons, details, evidence, and relationships between individuals, events, and ideas.

The Encyclopedia of Preserved People: Pickled, Frozen, and Mummified Corpses from Around the World
Natalie Jane Prior
1170L
ISBN: 978-0375822872
This text begins by explaining some of the differences between preserved bodies (mummies) and skeletons. This informational text presents basic facts and information in an engaging manner. Filled with images, illustrations, and full-color photographs, students can draw from multiple features to make meaning. There is a comprehensive index and bibliography included as well.

What a Beast! A Look-It-Up Guide to the Monsters and Mutants of Mythology
Sophia Kelly
920L
ISBN: 978-1606310601
This fun guide examines the fact and fiction of the stories associated with some of the most well-known beasts and creatures of lore. Readers learn specific facts about the origins of many of the stories and are introduced to lesser-known creatures as well. The bright colors, engaging photographs, and fun headings and captions make this a visually appealing text as well. This is a great text for multiple standards.

Word Play

"Words mean more than what is set down on paper. It takes the human voice to infuse them with shades of deeper meaning."
Maya Angelou, *poet*

READING INFORMATIONAL TEXT STANDARD 4:
WORD PLAY

Third	Fourth	Fifth
Determine the meaning of general academic and domain-specific words and phrases in a text relevant to a grade 3 topic or subject area.	Determine the meaning of general academic language and domain-specific words or phrases in a text relevant to a grade 4 topic or subject area.	Determine the meaning of general academic and domain-specific words and phrases in a text relevant to a grade 5 topic or subject area.

GRADE LEVEL DIFFERENCES

This standard is identical for each grade level. Students are focusing on determining the meaning of words within a grade-level text. This standard is not about spelling or defining words in isolation. Students are expected to pull vocabulary from the text and negotiate meaning.

The *Word Play* standard is about your students determining the meaning of words and phrases in context. *What happens when students encounter new words that they do not know? How do they negotiate text when there are phrases that they don't know?* Students need strategies to make meaning of unfamiliar words in order to construct larger textual meaning.

These strategies are not about words in isolation. They are about drawing on context clues to make decisions about the word. Consider your own reading. As adults we encounter words that we don't know all of the time. Do you read with a dictionary in hand? Is Bing or Google open so that you can stop and look up words each time you are unfamiliar? What is more likely is that readers rely on a set of virtually unconscious strategies to make sense of text.

Readers often have a set of strategies, a toolbox of sorts, which they draw from when they face unfamiliar words in a text. Your goal is to introduce students to more of these strategies. Common strategies that most teachers already rely on include: visualization, context clues, and definitions. There are two other strategies that are rarely explicitly taught: *word role* and *associations*. Consider adding these to your toolbox of strategies.

Word Role (Syntax)

The word role strategy is used when you get to a word or phrase that you don't know, but you know all of the other words in the sentence. You remove the word by covering it up to determine what role the word plays. *Is it describing (adjective)? Is it an action (verb)? Is it a thing (noun)?* This helps readers make some predictions about how the unfamiliar word is used in the sentence. An example: *Leslie had myriad interests in school.* As a reader, I may not know what *myriad* means. With the word role strategy, I would cover up *myriad* (physically or mentally). The new image of the sentence is now: *Leslie has BLANK interests in school.* This helps me notice that the unknown word is describing Leslie's interests. I still don't know that word, but I now know that it is used as an adjective. This also lets readers determine if they even need the word to understand the text or if they can continue reading and still grasp the meaning. I usually have students record these types of words; we explore these and add them to a class list of "special language." By the end of the year, students have a wall of words and phrases that they have learned from their reading and can now use in context.

Association

This strategy is about breaking the word up. In third through fifth grade, students will encounter words that are multisyllabic. Teach students to look for four things: roots, prefixes/suffixes, words within a word, and tone. The word *tone* may seem out of place here, but it is probably one of the most used in this set. When students see a word, they may not know the word well, but they may have seen parts of the word or recognize the word as being associated as a negative or positive concept. That association is what I call the tone of the word. Thinking about these associations may not reveal meaning, but it will get students critically thinking. To determine the tone of a word, students have to make connections to their own prior reading, background knowledge, and schema. This explicitly tells them to think! This is exactly what we want from any standard.

Key Point

Students need a set of strategies to make meaning of unfamiliar words to construct larger textual meaning.

90

1 *"Have you ever read a book and come across a word that you didn't know? I have! Well, what do you do when this happens?"* Discuss with students. Many will say that you look up the word. Point out that sometimes you can do that, but many times readers don't want to put their book down, get a dictionary and look up a word, then go back to the text. Explain that looking it up is a great habit, but that you want to give them a few other ways to think about words.

2 **Share with students that there are lots of ways to think about words.** *"Class, let me share a few ways that a reader can think about words."* Create an anchor chart (like the model here) with the eight different ways to think about word choice. I suggest introducing one or two at a time and building the list throughout the year.

3 **Select an informational text paragraph to read out loud to students.** Try to choose a passage with words that lend themselves to the word choice strategy that you are introducing. Ask students to try out one of the strategies on the list or just the one that you are introducing that day as you read. I like to have students keep a word log in their notebooks to keep a running list of words that we have explored in class, the strategy used, and the subsequent word meaning. I ask students to share with a partner or group, and then call on a few different students to share their word and discuss what it means.

4 **Repeat this as needed with each Word Play strategy.** I like to use this daily if I can. This is great for opening or closing the day or for those odd 10-minute periods before you transition to lunch or different activities.

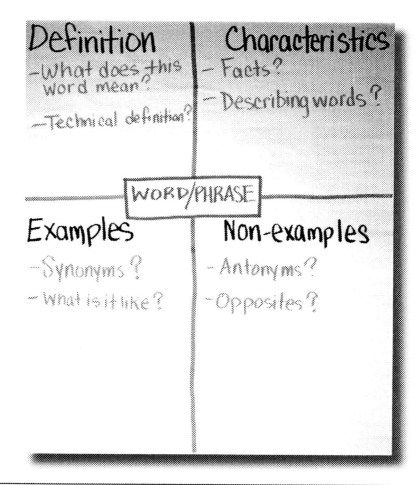

Modified Frayer anchor chart.

91

1 *"We've talked about how readers will often encounter words that they just don't know.* There are lots of things that readers do when they come across these types of words. Let's talk about some of these things." Review the anchor chart that you created when you introduced this standard and discuss it with students.

2 **Select a text that has domain- or content-specific words.** A science or social studies textbook is a great choice for this. Introduce the idea of vocabulary sentence frames. I like to use these to "nudge" students to explicitly think about challenging words. Use an example like the one I have here or create your own. There is no magic formula; the goal is to demand that critical conversations take place about words.

3 **Read the text out loud to students.** As you read, stop and identify vocabulary words that you are unsure about. At the end of the text, select one or two words to complete vocabulary sentence frames for. Think out loud as you complete your own frames, encouraging students to share ideas.

4 Set the expectation that students should think about words and create vocabulary sentence frames to share their thinking. A great idea is to post the frames in a special place in the room. Celebrate when students have a new word that they have found and completed a frame for. Over time, you can "shrink" the required information for the frames and eventually stop requiring them once students begin to autonomously think more critically about words.

Standard 4 : Sentence Frame

The word/phrase that I am thinking of is _____
(word/phrase from text)

It makes me think _____
(strategy)

The clues that I used _____
(textual evidence)

I checked with _____
(confirmation source)

I found out _____
(confirmation)

Vocabulary Sentence Frame anchor chart.

THE ORGANIZERS

After you have explicitly introduced and modeled how to apply the strategies of this standard to text, you want to provide students with an organizer that they can use to think about their own informational text reading. In order to make sure that students can independently understand and use the organizer, it is important to model how the specific organizer is used. Select a text and organizer of your choice. Complete the organizer with your students and post it as a model. Afterwards, students can independently use that same organizer multiple times to practice the skill with different informational texts. This can be done in pairs, groups, and independently.

The book that I use with each organizer in this chapter is *Moonshot* by Brian Floca. This book is used for each example for this standard for consistency and to offer the same book as a point of comparison for teachers.

1 Read (or reread) *Moonshot* to your students. If you don't have a copy for each student, project the text or use a document camera so that students can follow along and read it. As you talk with your students, be sure to use the language of this standard. Think out loud and complete the organizer together.

2 Once you model by explicitly completing the organizer, your students will understand the connection between the standard and the organizer. You can provide blank copies of the organizer and allow students to select their own informational text, assign one from your class anthology, or select a title from the suggested book list within this chapter.

3 Students can complete an organizer when they read any informational text. This can be done as an assignment and can be repeated as many times as you want with any informational text that you choose. The sky is the limit! This allows for multiple opportunities to tailor the text to the student and maintain fidelity to the standard.

4 Once students have demonstrated mastery of the skill, don't stop using it. You want your readers to keep practicing. In the introduction of the book, I discussed the pitfalls of being a Checklist Teacher. Students need to keep perfecting their skill sets.

5 Reuse the same organizer, make it into an anchor chart, or post exemplars for students to reference later. You can add the organizer to a standards-based center, pair it with your school's reading incentive program, or use it daily as evidence of reading.

CHECK & CONFIRM

This is a great choice from which to create a larger anchor chart. Students would benefit from seeing these questions when thinking about new vocabulary words.

I like this because students have lots of space to write and share their thinking.

Students can also identify how they confirmed the meaning. Dictionary? Another person? A website?

Check & Confirm

Word / Phrase

transearth injection

What I Think it Means . . .

putting something into the earth or pass it

Clues I Used . . .

I saw the word earth inside of the bigger word.
I know an injection is like a needle going in.

Check & Confirm Meaning . . .

This is used by spacecrafts when they are set on a path to reach earth.

Word / Phrase

What I Think it Means . . .

Clues I Used . . .

Check & Confirm Meaning . . .

Check & Confirm

DON'T BOX ME IN

We learned about *translunar* in the text. Students were eager to use that new learning to help make sense of this word.

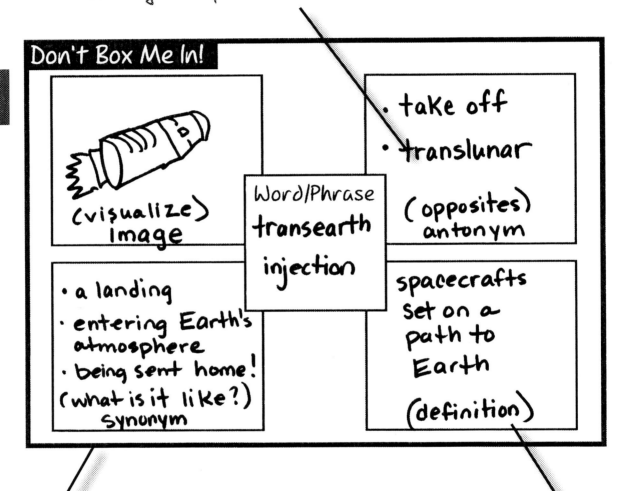

Don't Box Me In!

(visualize) Image

Word/Phrase
transearth
injection

• take off
• translunar

(opposites)
antonym

• a landing
• entering Earth's atmosphere
• being sent home!
(what is it like?)
Synonym

spacecrafts set on a path to Earth

(definition)

This is very similar to the Word Web organizer. The only difference is that your students can choose what they want to use each box for.

I encourage students to use the anchor chart for this standard to help them make choices about how they want to represent the word in each box.

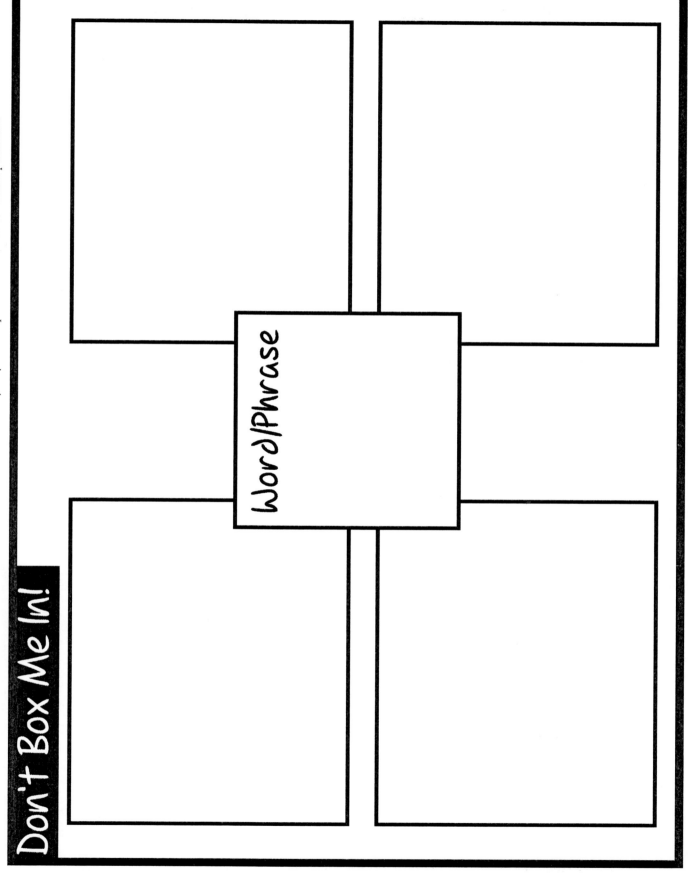

Word/Phrase

THINKING ABOUT WORDS

This works well with content- and domain-specific words.

I always complete the image first when I model this for students. They seem to think more about the words. This makes it is a great entry point to begin conversations about the word.

Thinking About Words

Word / Phrase

transearth injection

Synonym
- course to Earth
- landing
- entering Earth's atmosphere

Image

Antonym
- leaving earth
- liftoff
- on another planet

How I Can Use it in My Life:
- If I work for NASA I might be in charge of liftoffs and transearth injections.
- I am already on Earth so I don't need a transearth injection.

I complete this last and then lead a discussion about all of the possibilities for this section.

Thinking About Words

Word / Phrase

Synonym

Image

Antonym

How I Can Use it in My Life:

WORD USE

This presents a great opportunity to talk about ellipses and how they are used.

Word Use

Pg. #	Word / Phrase	Author's Use	My Use
front cover	transearth injection	... the CSM engine ignites for transearth injection.	Transearth injections send spacecrafts to earth.
front cover	translunar injection	...translunar injection pushing Apollo 11 out of orbit...	Translunar injections send objects away from the Earth.
9	ignition sequence	... ignition sequence started.	Spacecrafts have an ignition sequence before take off.
21	whir	...the whir of machines.	I hear the whir of the dishwasher at home.
25	craters	...safe site among the craters.	We have holes in the yard as big as craters.

Students can easily create a Word Use journal or recreate this form in a notebook.

Students usually enjoy creating personal sentences for new words. They often end up comical or upbeat.

Word Use

Pg. #	Word / Phrase	Author's Use	My Use

WORD WEB

WARNING!

This organizer is challenging for third graders. They often write very large and have challenges with the smaller space.

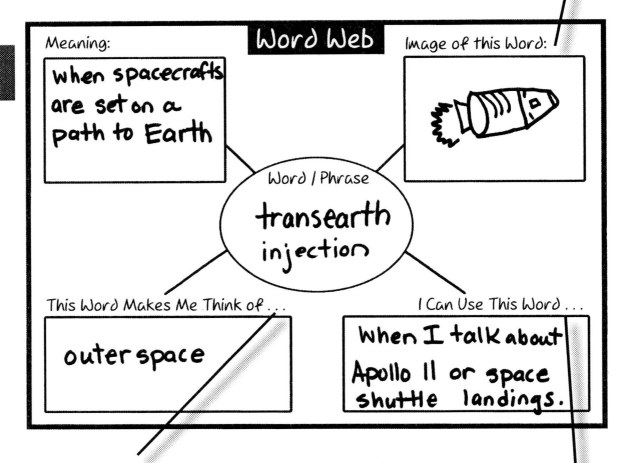

Word Web

Meaning:

when spacecrafts are set on a path to Earth

Image of this Word:

Word / Phrase

transearth injection

This Word Makes Me Think of . . .

outer space

I Can Use This Word . . .

When I talk about Apollo 11 or space shuttle landings.

Note the use of the ellipses again. Teach students when this is an effective practice. This is important for note-taking in other contexts as well.

This organizer can be used as-is, or you can just use the headings and ask students to respond to those on paper.

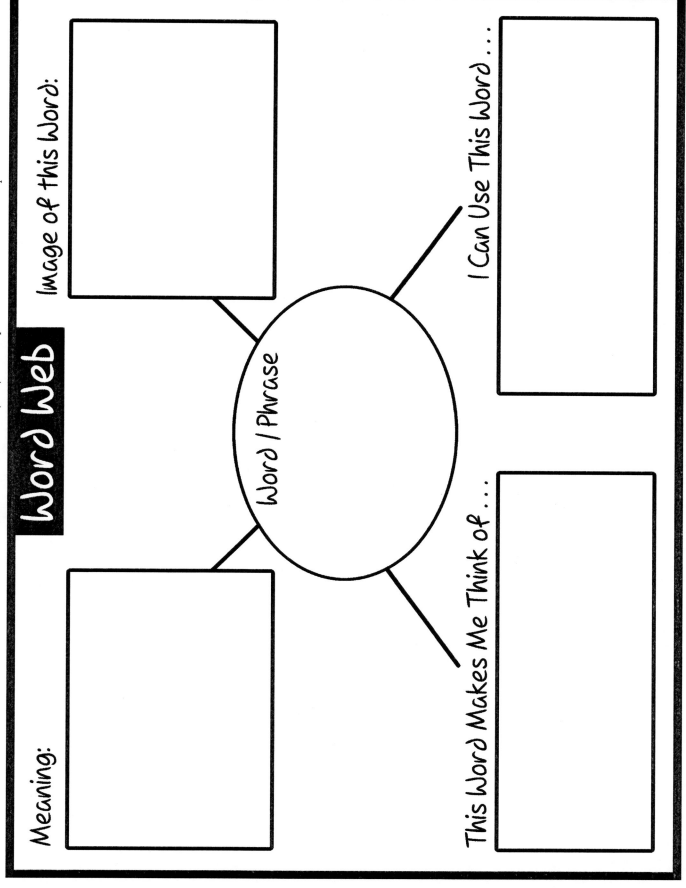

Word Web

Image of this Word:

Meaning:

Word / Phrase

I Can Use This Word...

This Word Makes Me Think of...

AMERICAN HISTORY

A History of the People: All the People, 1945–2001
Joy Hakim
940L
ISBN: 978-0195153385
This text explores the political and social transitions of this time period. Students learn about major wars such as the Cold War, Vietnam, and the War on Terror. The text also uses photographs of firsthand documents to explain the Declaration of Independence, the Constitution, and the Bill of Rights. Rich images, sidebars, and multiple text structures are throughout the text. Multiple thematic issues are addressed in terms of equality, segregation, and freedom.

Abraham Lincoln and Frederick Douglass: The Story Behind an American Friendship
Russell Freedman
1110L
ISBN: 978-0547385624
Freedman, the author of *Lincoln: A Photobiography,* introduces readers to the parallel lives of these two men. Readers learn how both men grew up poor, were self-educated, and considered slavery morally wrong. Freedman does not gloss over the racial differences and Lincoln's initial avoidance of the Civil War, despite the consequences it would have for slavery. Well thought-out, rich in details, and thought-provoking, this 128-page text is most appropriate for readers who have built up stamina for longer texts. Freedman includes his own final notes, a bibliography, and an index.

African-Americans in the Thirteen Colonies
Deborah Kent
990L
ISBN: 978-0516200651
Kent's moving book shares the facts about a time period when African-Americans are rarely mentioned in most social studies textbooks. Readers learn how the first Africans came to the colonies and worked alongside Europeans. Kent shares the history of contributions made by these workers, the evolution of their roles in the colonies, and the eventual system of slavery that resulted. This book is poignant and informative.

The Dreadful, Smelly Colonies
Elizabeth Raum
810L
ISBN: 978-1429663519
This text explores the difficulties of life in the thirteen colonies. Readers learn why colonists

had to resort to a wide range of practices that we would consider dangerous and unsanitary today. This book is a great match for both your history buffs and lovers of all things gross.

The Fourth of July Story
Alice Dalgliesh
790L
ISBN: 978-0689718762

This 32-page book explains the history of the United States in a narrative format. Students learn factual information in a tone that feels very much like a conversation with the author. Organized into chapters, the book also includes rich illustrations on virtually every page.

The New Americans: Colonial Times: 1620–1689
Betsy Maestro
940L
ISBN: 978-0060575724

In this 48-page book, readers learn about the different European countries that explored the New World and the resulting colonies. Rich watercolors fill most pages, often covering the whole page, with the text set right inside. Readers will encounter content-specific vocabulary and a wealth of details about colonial life.

The Real Story About Government and Politics in Colonial America
Kristine Carlson Asselin
720L
ISBN: 978-1429672191

This text explores the difficult life of the colonial era. Instead of whitewashing the period, the text tackles some of the strange things that went on in the colonies. Students learn about morbid medical practices as well as the use of whippings as punishments. The text focuses on the strains of British rule and the eventual fight for independence. The book also includes a wide range of illustrations and paintings.

ANIMALS

Do Tarantulas Have Teeth? Questions and Answers About Poisonous Creatures
Jim Effler, Gilda Berger, and Melvin Berger
730L
ISBN: 978-0606195546

This informational text is a must-read for the snake and spider lover in your classroom. One of the great features of the question-and-answer format in this book is that the questions all sound like they were posed by actual elementary school students. Answers to questions like, *"What happens when an enemy bites off a spider's leg?"* are featured throughout this text. Detailed text features include varied headings, vivid paintings and photographs, facts, figures, and charts. Students are exposed to content-specific vocabulary and a wide variety of details and facts about the characteristics of over twenty-two different species of poisonous insects and reptiles.

Dogs
Seymour Simon
870L
ISBN: 978-0064462556

This book is a hit with younger children because it explores an animal that most are fond of. Simple and straightforward, Simon's text is written for a pretty young audience. The words are easy to decode and images help explain the text and descriptions featured throughout the book. The photographs are touching and vivid, including several two-page spreads. Simon describes the birth and growth of animals, with numerous images of puppies and dogs of different breeds. This is great introduction to informational text for students who are used to fiction. It is nonthreatening and offers a fun, easily accessible entry point for young readers.

Dolphin Adventure: A True Story
Wayne Grover and Jim Fowler
930L
ISBN: 978-0380732524

This is a firsthand account of Grover's experience with a dolphin family off the coast of Florida. Grover chronicles how he first encountered the dolphin family. He also explains how he came to perform underwater surgery with his diving knife, saving one of the dolphins from dying. Later, one of the dolphins saves Grover from two sharks. Grover does a great job of explaining his feelings and documenting the experience. This is a great text to consider when sharing an example of a firsthand text.

How Do Frogs Swallow with Their Eyes? Questions and Answers About Amphibians
Gilda Berger and Melvin Berger
610L
ISBN: 978-0439266772

This text is organized to answer a series of questions about amphibians. The reader is introduced to the question-and-answer format, along with the concept of guiding questions. The text asks a wide range and type of questions such as: *"What is an amphibian's best defense?"* and *"How do frogs swallow with their eyes?"* While this text is easy to read, it does feature content-specific words like *metamorphosis*.

True Tales of Animal Heroes
Allan Zullo
780L
ISBN: 978-0816772469

This informational text features a wide variety of animals that have saved the lives of their owners. Each story includes a variety of text features. The photographs and engaging tales are well-suited to the reluctant reader. Highly decodable text makes this book an excellent choice for third graders and struggling fourth and fifth graders. This is also a great choice for modeling.

Who Are You Calling a Woolly Mammoth?
Elizabeth Levy
970L
ISBN: 978-0590129381

This 128-page informational text uses humor and jokes to take the reader on a chronological journey through the prehistoric period. Readers learn not just about the woolly mammoth but about nine additional animals that lived during the Ice Age. This book is a great choice for the Word Play and Text Structure standards. This text is also effective for exploring main idea, details, and sequential order.

BIOGRAPHY/ AUTOBIOGRAPHY/ MEMOIR

Louis Braille, The Boy Who Invented Books for the Blind
Margaret Davidson
510L
ISBN: 978-0590443500

This biography traces the life of this 19th-century inventor. Readers learn about how the Braille system was invented and the context of the invention. This is an excellent text to support instruction on time sequence, main ideas, and summarizing.

Father Abraham: Lincoln and His Sons
Harold Holzer
1060L
ISBN: 978-1590783030

This 232-page chapter book is most appropriate for your advanced readers who have built stamina for longer independent reading. Fifth graders will enjoy reading a less common narrative of Lincoln. This text, organized into fifteen chapters, examines Lincoln's relationships with his four sons. Black-and-white images of Lincoln, his sons, and places that the Lincolns lived are found throughout the text. Readers have multiple opportunities to think critically about relationships, events, and ideas in this text.

Mr. Blue Jeans: A Story About Levi Strauss
Maryann N. Weidt
960L
ISBN: 978-0876145883

Readers are introduced to the man behind the Levi Jeans company. The text details the humble beginnings of his life as a Jewish immigrant. Readers make sense of the text through multiple text features including captions, an index, bibliography, maps, and images. This is an appropriate text to reinforce multiple standards.

107

Steve Jobs: Think Differently
Patricia Lakin
940L
ISBN: 978-1442453937
Written by a former elementary school teacher, this biography profiles Jobs and his work at Apple and Pixar. Readers learn of his adoptive parents, early life, and inventions. Jobs is portrayed as a rule-breaker who turned his curiosity and creativity into an empire. At 192 pages, this is most appropriate for your stronger readers.

When Marian Sang: The True Recital of Marian Anderson, the Voice of the Century
Pam Muñoz Ryan
780L
ISBN: 978-0439269674
This biographical text, illustrated by Brian Selznick (*Frindle*), pairs beautiful imagery with narrative storytelling. Ryan details the challenges that Marian Anderson faced as a singer in the racially charged 1930's. Ryan details the overt racism and discrimination that prevented Anderson from being able to perform in some parts of America because of her ethnicity. Filled with beautiful sepia images, a discography, and timeline, this text offers numerous details and text features to engage readers. The text ends with a wordless painting of Anderson finally singing at the Lincoln Memorial during a historic 1939 concert before an integrated audience of almost 80,000 people.

ENVIRONMENT

A River Ran Wild: An Environmental History
Lynne Cherry
670L
ISBN: 978-0152163723
This text explores the ecology of New England's Nashua River. Cherry details how the river went from being cherished by generations of Native Americans to becoming a polluted wasteland, devoid of plentiful fish and wildlife, in the 1960's. The book offers an honest and detailed history of the Nashua River. The ideas are complex and the illustrations tell the story as effectively as the text. She includes a timeline, maps, and additional text features to support the argument that water pollution can have a catastrophic impact on nature.

Far From Shore: Chronicles of an Open Ocean Voyage
Sophie Webb
1030L
ISBN: 978-0618597291
Readers travel with a young biologist on her adventures. Rich blue pages feature vivid illustrations of dolphins and flying fish, while wonderful text features such as captions, maps, sidebars, diagrams, and charts are found on most pages. This text includes a wide variety of details about the tools and resources that biologists use along with information about the varied creatures that they encounter.

The Most Beautiful Roof in the World: Exploring the Rainforest Canopy
Kathryn Lasky and Christopher G. Knight
1160L
ISBN: 978-0152008970

This 48-page informational text focuses on the rainforest canopy. Students follow biologist Meg Lowman and her assistant as they explore and document the plant and animal life found in the Belize rainforest canopy. The authors explain the specific methods that scientists use to conduct research and collect specimens and samples from the rainforest. The text also documents Lowman's relationship with her two sons, who have come along on her adventure. This book is definitely geared more towards your fifth graders and can be challenging, despite its relatively short length.

Scholastic Question & Answer: What Makes an Ocean Wave?
John Rice, Gilda Berger and Melvin Berger
870L
ISBN: 978-0439148825

I find that this book is most engaging for third graders. Students are introduced to a simple question-and-answer format, but with the familiar feel of a picture book. A simple question is asked, followed by a series of facts, images, and text that respond to the question. This book is part of the Scholastic *Question & Answer* series. These science-centered books all focus on different topics, most filled with great physical text features and images. There are multiple other books in this series that explore the solar system, whales, tornadoes, and butterflies.

Tornado: Nature in Action
Stephen Kramer
940L
ISBN: 978-1575050584

This text examines the dangers of a tornado. Up-close photographs of the devastation and aftermath of tornadoes are included throughout the text. Readers learn what happens inside of storm clouds and practical ways to stay safe. Readers can identify main ideas and connections with this book. The wealth of maps, charts, graphs, and tables make this an appropriate choice for text structure.

Volcanoes
Seymour Simon
880L
ISBN: 978-0060877170

The deep, rich photographs found here are enough to draw most readers into this text. Spewing lava and erupting mountains fill about half of the pages of this text. Readers will encounter a wide variety of content-specific vocabulary and organizational structures. This text works well to reinforce multiple informational text standards.

Mummies, Monsters, and Creatures

Cat Mummies
Kelly Trumble
870L
ISBN: 978-0395968918
This engaging chapter book shows how Egyptian mummification was not just for humans. The author uses color-washed illustrations to walk readers through the reasons why cats were sacred to Egyptians, how they were mummified, and the thousands of cat mummies that have been found.

Fantastical Creatures and Magical Beasts
Shannon Knudsen
870L
ISBN: 978-0822599876
This 48-page book is a good mix of fantasy and informational text. While the topic of imaginary beasts usually leads to fictional reading, this text handles it differently. Readers learn the fictitious stories of numerous magical creatures, but learn the real story behind the myth. This is an excellent choice for students who enjoy fantasy. Rich colors, narrative-style writing, and succinct chapters make this a solid choice for many different types of readers.

The Loch Ness Monster (Solving Mysteries with Science)
Lori Hile
1050L
ISBN: 978-1410949929
Hile uses the scientific method to determine if the Loch Ness monster ever really existed. Detailing the myths surrounding the Loch Ness monster, Hile takes readers on a scientific exploration where mystery and fiction meet science and discovery. This text includes charts, graphs, suggested web resources, call-out boxes, a glossary, and an index.

Mummies of the Pharaohs
Melvin Berger and Gilda Berger
1000L
ISBN: 978-0439335959
Written in the informative, yet accessible style that the Bergers are known for, this text is packed with information. Readers are introduced to King Tut, Ramses II, and a wide variety of other well-known and lesser-known Egyptian mummies. There are large, colorful photographs found on almost every page. This 64-page book comes in hardcover and paperback; the paperback version is often difficult to locate, but both editions have the same information.

What a Beast! A Look-It-Up Guide to the Monsters and Mutants of Mythology
Sophia Kelly
920L
ISBN: 978-1606310601

This fun guide examines the fact and fiction of the stories associated with some of the most well-known beasts and creatures of lore. Readers learn specific facts about the origins of many of the stories and are introduced to lesser-known creatures as well. The bright colors, engaging photographs, and fun headings and captions make this a visually appealing text as well. This is a great text for multiple standards.

OUTER SPACE

Galaxies
Seymour Simon
1010L
ISBN: 978-0688109929

This book is written in the informative style that Simon has become known for. The book features deep colors and images that vividly complement the text. Readers learn about the Milky Way and different categories of galaxies. This text can be used with any informational text standard.

Jupiter
Seymour Simon
820L
ISBN: 978-0064437592

This text is well-written and informative. Readers learn about Jupiter through rich photographs and detailed descriptions. The text is a great introduction to Jupiter and complimentary to many science units in these grades.

Moonshot
Brian Floca
990L
ISBN: 978-1416950462

This text traces the preparation for and the flight of Apollo 11 in 1969. The vivid colors and familiar picture-book style make this text an engaging and visually inviting choice for young readers. This is an appropriate choice when exploring main ideas, details, connections, and summarizing.

The Solar System
Laura Hamilton Waxman
650L
ISBN: 978-0761338741

This 48-page book is organized into six chapters. Chapters are typically less than ten pages long. Each page features vivid images and colorful, large print. An index, glossary, and suggested resources to learn more about the solar system are also included.

Thirteen Planets

David Aguilar

1120L

ISBN: 978-1426307706

This 64-page informational text is published by *National Geographic*. Organized as more of a reference book, this text discusses the redefinition of the word *planet,* explores the three dwarf planets, and explains about comets and asteroids. The images are stunning and vivid. Readers can explore multiple text structures and encounter a wide range of content-specific vocabulary.

Text Structure

"It's not wise to violate the rules until you know how to observe them."
T. S. Eliot, *poet*

READING INFORMATIONAL TEXT STANDARD 5:
TEXT STRUCTURE

Third	Fourth	Fifth
Use text features and search tools (e.g., key words, sidebars, hyperlinks) to locate information relevant to a given topic quickly and efficiently.	Describe the overall structure (e.g., chronology, comparison, cause/effect, problem/solution) of events, ideas, concepts, or information in a text or part of a text.	Compare and contrast the overall structure (e.g., chronology, comparison, cause/effect, problem/solution) of events, ideas, concepts, or information in two or more texts.

GRADE LEVEL DIFFERENCES

When teaching the Text Structure standard there are two different areas to consider: *physical text features* and *organizational structures/features*. Each grade level focuses on a specific aspect of the standard. In third grade, students are expected to understand the physical text features. These include hyperlinks, bullets, headings, sidebars, chart, graphs, etc. In fourth and fifth grade, the focus is no longer on physical text features; students are expected to look at the organizational structures of the text. In fifth grade, students continue to look at the organizational structures of the text, but expand the focus to include multiple texts.

Students in third through fifth grade have probably spent several years learning about narrative structure. As they begin to learn more about informational text, they have to reframe how they think about text because **informational text can be nonlinear.** This means that it does not have to be read in the same way by everyone. Readers can "enter" the text in multiple ways. This is particularly true for digital text. Think about a website: one reader might navigate the content very differently than another reader. The *entry points* are different. This standard demands that students recognize the different entry points and what functions they serve. These entry points are the text structures, and these structures can be *physical* or *organizational*.

Third Grade
Third graders are only required to recognize the *physical text structures*. Examples include **key words, bullets, sidebars, hyperlinks** or **subtitles.** Consider these structures to be what you see when you open up a book or a website. *What is physically there to organize the words?*

Fourth and Fifth Grade
Fourth and fifth graders focus on the *organizational structures*. These include **patterns of time sequence (chronological order), problem/solution, description, comparison, and cause/effect.** Fourth graders need to recognize and describe these structures. Fifth graders need to recognize these structures and compare them across texts. Please note that the standards do make the assumption that your fourth and fifth graders have already mastered the physical structures. In many cases you may want to explicitly teach both types in those grade levels as well.

These are some of the common organization structures that students need to be able to describe (fourth grade) and compare across texts (fifth grade):

1. Time Sequence
These sections of text are organized to sequentially unfold as a series of events, steps, or ideas. This structure follows a chronological order.

2. Problem/Solution
Authors present a problem and offer a way to fix that problem.

3. Description
Authors explain a phenomenon, event, idea, or person. This is often relegated to one section. Rarely is the overall purpose of a piece solely to describe.

4. Compare/Contrast
Authors explain how two or more things are alike or different. This type of structure lends itself to entire pieces, but also to sections of information that have a larger, different purpose. Look for call-outs or images to depend on this structure as well.

5. Cause/Effect
Authors present causal relationships. These can extend to multiple subjects, ideas, and events.

It is important to note that a text can include elements from several of the organizational structures listed above. The language of the standards, however, asks students to look for the overall structure of the text. This is what is most predominant.

1 **Ask students to think about the kinds of jobs that they want to have when they grow up.** Call on student volunteers to share their career choices with the class.

2 **Explain that just like people have jobs, so do the pieces of an informational text.** Each sentence, paragraph, image, or section plays a role in helping the readers understand the text. *"Well, since you guys have shared a bit about the roles you want to take on in the future, let me talk about how that relates to reading informational text. Each part has a role or job. There are no coincidences or sections that are just there for no reason at all. Each piece has a job, a role, a structure, and a function."*

3 **Create a Text Structure anchor chart, like the one pictured here, that displays the different roles that informational text sections can have.** Many people refer to these as *organizational structures*. I like to think of *structures* as the umbrella term. These can include physical features *and* organizational features. Students can rely on this anchor chart throughout the year when analyzing text.

4 **Introduce models of each structure.** You want to use short paragraphs or text excerpts to do this. A great strategy is to use a science or social studies text or a basal reader. Each of these structures can easily be found in short, easy formats. I select a few textbooks and place a sticky note during my planning on the places where I notice specific structures, then I photocopy or provide the text for the students to read as we study each one.

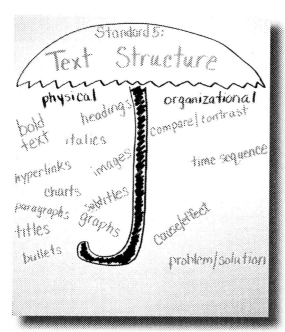

This is a fourth and fifth grade Text Structure anchor chart that features both physical and organizational structures.

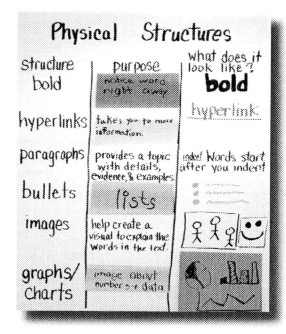

Third grade anchor chart featuring common physical text structures

1 **Select examples of informational text that match each of the different structures you introduced earlier.** Note: fourth and fifth grade will focus on the *organizational structures*. Third grade will focus on *physical structures*. I find that it is easiest to pull these from online news sources or photocopy a page from an anthology that shows the structure. Another quick and accurate source is a science or social studies book. These texts are rich with graphics and multiple entry points for the reader. It is easy to do a visual scan and select an excerpt that is organized in multiple ways. For this lesson it is not important just yet that students identify different organizational structures within a larger text. You are still helping them to conceptualize the structures, so a small excerpt is appropriate.

For third graders focusing on physical structures, the *Text Structure* standard could be taught in conjunction with the *Beyond Text* standard. Both look at the physical features and how they help readers.

2 **Read each of your selected text excerpts aloud with the students.** After you read each one, discuss what type of structure you noted. *What function did it serve? How does it work?* Ask students to engage with you as you try to encourage a discussion about each excerpt. Make sure that you classify each of the excerpts to the corresponding text structure and function.

3 **Refer back to your initial anchor chart.** Consider letting your students add visual representations of each structure to the anchor chart as well. Students could even create their own charts as you introduce and model each feature. This can be ongoing throughout the year or taught as a longer unit that introduces each structure.

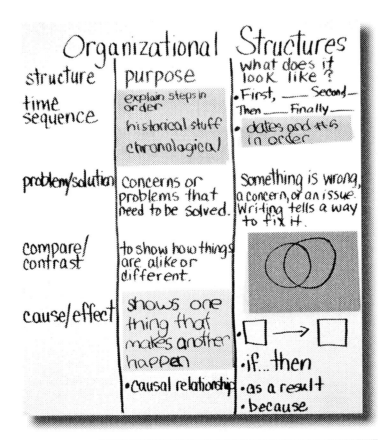

Students added information for several of the categories for this anchor chart. It is organized by the organizational features/structures.

The Organizers

After you have explicitly introduced and modeled how to apply the strategies of this standard to text, you want to provide students with an organizer that they can use to think about their own informational text reading. In order to make sure that students can independently understand and use the organizer, it is important to model how the specific organizer is used. Select a text and organizer of your choice. Complete the organizer with your students and post it as a model. Afterwards, students can independently use that same organizer multiple times to practice the skill with different informational texts. This can be done in pairs, groups, and independently.

The books that I use with each organizer in this chapter are *Team Moon: How 400,000 People Landed Apollo 11 on the Moon* by Catherine Thimmesh and *Moonshot* by Brian Floca. One of these two books is used for each example for this standard for consistency and to offer the same book as a point of comparison for teachers.

1 Read (or reread) the text to your students. If you don't have a copy for each student, project the text or use a document camera so that students can follow along and read it. As you talk with your students, be sure to use the language of this standard. Think out loud and complete the organizer together.

2 Once you model by explicitly completing the organizer, your students will understand the connection between the standard and the organizer. You can provide blank copies of the organizer and allow students to select their own informational text, assign one from your class anthology, or select a title from the suggested book list within this chapter.

3 Students can complete an organizer when they read any informational text. This can be done as an assignment and can be repeated as many times as you want with any informational text that you choose. The sky is the limit! This allows for multiple opportunities to tailor the text to the student and maintain fidelity to the standard.

4 Once students have demonstrated mastery of the skill, don't stop using it. You want your readers to keep practicing. In the introduction of the book, I discussed the pitfalls of being a Checklist Teacher. Students need to keep perfecting their skill sets.

5 Reuse the same organizer, make it into an anchor chart, or post exemplars for students to reference later. You can add the organizer to a standards-based center, pair it with your school's reading incentive program, or use it daily as evidence of reading.

COMPARING STRUCTURE

This graphic organizer matches the requirements for fifth grade, but can be used with any grade level.

	Text 1:	Text 2:
Text Title	Moonshot	Team Moon
Structure	Illustrations with captions	Call-out boxes with definitions
How this structure helped readers:	- The spacecraft, the moon, and the astronauts are all illustrated and labeled so you can make a picture in your mind.	This helps explain the confusing words and even gives examples so you understand what you are reading.

Comparing Structure

I deliberately did not indicate which structure students look for here. This can be organizational or physical.

This can also be cut down the center or folded in half to examine one text at a time.

Comparing Structure

	Text 1:	Text 2:
Text Title		
Structure		
How this structure helped readers:		

FEATURE CHART

This graphic organizer is designed for third graders and focuses on physical features.

This question is essential for students. They really have to critically think to determine how a feature helps readers.

Feature Chart

Text Feature	Information	How does this make the text easier to understand?
Labeled Space Shuttle	You learn what all of the parts are on a spacecraft	You really 'get' how complicated the spacecraft is.
Bold Words	They stand out and have explanations written underneath.	You don't miss out on the big things.
Names written in italics	Columbia and the Eagle are both written in italics.	You always notice it and know it is the spacecraft.
Drawings of the moon	The craters and darkness.	You can visualize their discoveries.

As I think out loud with the students, I often "upgrade" my vocabulary and let them hear me do this. I went through several choices, out loud, before selecting "discoveries."

Feature Chart

Text Feature	Information	How does this make the text easier to understand?

FEATURES & TOOLS

I use the word "tools" here because I want students to see these different features as tools for them to make sense of text.

Features & Tools	Text: Moonshot
Features / Tools	What I Learned:
Illustrated and labeled picture of the Apollo spacecraft.	All of the parts and the purposes of the different spacecraft pieces.
Pictures in the story next to words.	Visualize what the words look like. Paints a picture in my mind.
Bold words in capital letters.	Important vocabulary and scientific words I need to know.
Illustrated timeline	Each step followed to launch the astronauts into space.
Subtitle: The Flight of Apollo 11.	What the book was really about.

Share what a subtitle is with students. I find this is a great feature that they can understand and use in their own writing.

I like to point out comprehension strategies that I used and share with students.

Features & Tools

Text: _____

Features / Tools	What I Learned:

POST THAT STRUCTURE

Writing Connection

This can become a great planner for a written summary.

Post That Structure!

Which OVERALL structure do you see?

☐ Problem / Solution ☐ Cause / Effect
☒ Chronology ☐ Compare & Contrast

Use sticky notes to organize how events were explained in this text:

First, Astronauts get their special clothing and helmets.

Then, They board the Columbia and the Eagle.

Mission control prepares for the lift off.

Afterwards, It's Liftoff!

Finally, The transearth injection returns them to Earth.

The explore space and look at everything.

Next, Astronauts live in the space craft for one week.

This turned into a great opportunity to discuss transitional words.

I cut larger sticky notes down to size. Use the smallest ones that your students can write on. This forces them to only include one event at a time.

Post That Structure!

Which OVERALL structure do you see?

☐ Problem / Solution ☐ Cause / Effect

☐ Chronology ☐ Compare & Contrast

Use sticky notes to organize how events were explained in this text:

VISUALIZING STRUCTURE

This is an appropriate choice when you first model a structure or introduce it. Students should not continue to use this when they advance beyond the initial understanding of the structure.

126

Text Title: **Moonshot**

What is the OVERALL structure of this text?

☐ Cause / Effect   ☒ Chronology
☐ Problem / Solution   ☐ Comparison

Illustrate this structure.

$1 \Rightarrow 2 \Rightarrow 3 \Rightarrow 4$

Explain your illustration below.

The story goes in order. You learn how it happens by reading what happened first, second, and third. That is just like my illustration.

Visualizing Structure

This space can also be used for students to form a sentence that explains the structure, in addition to just checking the box.

Kids love to think of how to visualize a structure. This is often a creative and fun part to work on.

Text Title: _____

What is the OVERALL structure of this text?

☐ Cause / Effect   ☐ Chronology

☐ Problem / Solution   ☐ Comparison

Illustrate this structure.

Explain your illustration below.

Visualizing Structure

ANIMALS

A River Ran Wild: An Environmental History
Lynne Cherry
670L
ISBN: 978-0152163723

This text explores the ecology of New England's Nashua River. Cherry details how the river went from being cherished by generations of Native Americans to becoming a polluted wasteland, devoid of plentiful fish and wildlife, in the 1960's. The book offers an honest and detailed history of the Nashua River. The ideas are complex and the illustrations tell the story as effectively as the text. She includes a timeline, maps, and additional text features to support the argument that water pollution can have a catastrophic impact on nature.

Animals Nobody Loves
Seymour Simon
860L
ISBN: 978-1587171550

This engaging text pairs vivid images and photographs with interesting and informative facts about 20 different animals. This text works well when teaching students to summarize and identify main ideas and details.

Big Cats
Seymour Simon
1050L
ISBN: 978-0064461191

This award-winning book (*Outstanding Science Trade Books for Children Award*) is all about the different types of cats of the animal kingdom. The text has vivid photographs of jaguars, cheetahs, lions, and pumas. The animal lover in your class will be drawn to this text, as it details how these animals hunt, raise their young, and make their homes. It offers numerous opportunities to examine images and other physical text features for details.

Do Tarantulas Have Teeth? Questions and Answers About Poisonous Creatures
Jim Effler, Gilda Berger and Melvin Berger
730L
ISBN: 978-0606195546

This informational text is a must-read for the snake and spider lover in your classroom. One of the great features of the question-and-answer format in this book is that the questions all sound like they were posed by actual elementary school students. Answers to questions like: *"What happens when an enemy bites off a spider's leg?"* are featured throughout this text. Detailed text features include varied headings, vivid paintings and photographs, facts, figures, and charts. Students are exposed to content-specific vocabulary and a wide variety of details and facts about the characteristics of over 22 different species of poisonous insects and reptiles.

Dogs
Seymour Simon
870L
ISBN: 978-0064462556

This book is a hit with younger children because it explores an animal that most are fond of. Simple and straightforward, Simon's text is written for a pretty young audience. The words are easy to decode and images help explain the text. There are detailed descriptions featured throughout the book. The photographs are touching and vivid, including several two-page spreads. Simon describes the birth and growth of animals, with numerous images of puppies and dogs of different breeds. This is a great introduction to informational text for students who are used to fiction; it is nonthreatening and offers a fun, easily accessible entry point for young readers.

How Do Frogs Swallow with Their Eyes? Questions and Answers About Amphibians
Gilda Berger and Melvin Berger
610L
ISBN: 978-0439266772

This text is organized to answer a series of questions about amphibians. The reader is introduced to the question-and-answer format, along with the concept of guiding questions. The text asks a wide range and type of questions such as *"What is an amphibian's best defense?"* and *"How do frogs swallow with their eyes?"* While this text is easy to read, it does feature content-specific words like *metamorphosis*.

Outside and Inside Snakes
Sandra Markle
830L
ISBN: 978-0780783348

This informational text provides a great deal of facts, descriptions and details about snakes. The text has a strong focus on snake anatomy, hunting and feeding techniques and how venom works. Detailed descriptions of the snakes' digestive and respiratory systems rely on content-specific words and provide multiple opportunities to practice the Word Play standard. The text is also effective at crafting comparison and contrast opportunities between humans and snakes. The vivid images, diagrams, and captions offer opportunities to examine physical text structure of informational text as well.

Stegosaurus
Elaine Landau
860L
ISBN: 978-0531154748

This text is an accessible choice for examining text structures. Landau crafts an investigative text through the use of an index, glossary, and sidebars. A section called "To Find Out More" provides students with additional resources, books, and hyperlinks to internet sites about the stegosaurus and other dinosaurs.

Talented Animals: A Chapter Book

Mary Packard

630L

ISBN: 978-0516244617

This book is a great choice for third graders. The book details the experiences of different animals with unique talents. These include a wide variety of animals, such as Tillie, a dog who paints, and Koko, the gorilla who uses sign language. This book is filled with colorful photographs, captions, an index, and a wide variety of physical text structures.

True Tales of Animal Heroes

Allan Zullo

780L

ISBN: 978-0816772469

This informational text features a wide variety of animals that have saved the lives of their owners. Each story includes a variety of text features. The photographs and engaging tales are well-suited to the reluctant reader. Highly decodable text makes this book an excellent choice for third graders and struggling fourth and fifth graders.

BIOGRAPHY/ AUTOBIOGRAPHY/ MEMOIR

Amelia to Zora

Cynthia Chin-Lee

1040L

ISBN: 978-1570915239

This 32-page book features one-page biographies of 26 different women. Each biography is organized alphabetically by first name. Some of the women included are: Lena Horne, Jane Goodall, Kristi Yamaguchi, Oprah Winfrey, and Mother Teresa. Illustrations and paintings are found throughout the book. Readers are able to draw inferences about each woman and point to supporting textual evidence for their choices.

End Zone

Tiki Barber and Ronde Barber

830L

ISBN: 978-1416990970

This heart-warming book is one of my personal favorites to read out loud with my students. Football fans and students with siblings, in particular, will be drawn to this tale of brothers who lead their junior high teammates to a state football championship. Both grow up to be real-life professional football players. The text offers quite a few opportunities to make connections between individuals, ideas, and events.

We Are the Ship

Kadir Nelson

900L

ISBN: 978-0786808328

This text contains biographical elements, but really tells the story of the Negro Baseball

League. Biographical vignettes of players are woven throughout, but the narrative structure really weaves a tale of determination, history, and sacrifice. Vivid colors and engaging descriptions are found throughout the book. This text offers multiple opportunities to ask questions and think critically about individuals, ideas, and events.

The Amazing Harry Kellar: Great American Magician
Gail Jarrow
910L
ISBN: 978-1590788653
Kellar is described as the first internationally famous magician. Readers learn of Kellar's relationship to Harry Houdini and *The Wizard of Oz*. The 96-page text examines misconceptions about magicians and early beliefs that they were really wizards or demonic. Black-and-white photographs, posters, and drawings help bring a sense of authenticity to this text. Readers will have multiple opportunities to examine causal relationships, main ideas, and relationships between ideas, events, and individuals.

Steve Jobs & Steve Wozniak: Geek Heroes Who Put the Personal in Computers
Mike Venezia
940L
ISBN: 978-0531223512
This 32-page book is filled with cartoon-style drawings, black-and-white photographs, and colorful images. Readers learn about the pioneers behind the Apple brand. Multiple text features such as an index, glossary, captions, and sidebars are included throughout. This is most appropriate for your younger readers.

Stealing Home: The Story of Jackie Robinson
Barry Denenberg
930L
ISBN: 978-0590425605
Filled with black-and-white photographs, this text is engaging and detailed. Readers have multiple opportunities to make inferences and support them with details and ideas from the text. This is an engaging text for most students, particularly your baseball fans.

INVENTIONS/ INVENTORS

High-Tech Inventions: A Chapter Book
Mary Packard
770L
ISBN: 978-0516246840
This short chapter book explores inventions that are as varied as the first computer to a remote-controlled cockroach. A collection of short stories about technological inventions, this text has captions, photos, sidebars, an index, and glossary.

The Kid Who Invented the Popsicle: And Other Surprising Stories About Inventions
Don Wulffson
1080L
ISBN: 978-0141302041

This book is my absolute favorite to use for any type of modeling. The short informational text lends itself to both being read out loud or independently. I also enjoy that the topics are all presented on one page. This allows you to read and discuss an entire invention with your students rather than just an excerpt. Written by Don Wulffson, who is known for his writing on kid-friendly inventions, the text has his trademark fun writing style and quirky introduction to facts and details. The text includes a wide variety of facts that most adults don't know. Fully engaging and just plain fun, this text can be used for multiple standards.

Toys! Amazing Stories Behind Some Great Inventions
Don Wulffson
920L
ISBN: 978-0805061963

This text is such an engaging collection of short informational text essays. Organized to read like short articles, each section of this book explains the origin of a different type of toy. Over 25 different toys are featured here, including Mr. Potato Head, Raggedy Ann, Twister, Silly Putty, and Trivial Pursuit. Students will devour the content and stay engaged with the text.

MUMMIES, MONSTERS, AND CREATURES

Bizarre Dinosaurs
National Geographic Society
1020L
ISBN: 978-1426303302

This well-crafted book uses information from paleontologist Josh Smith to inform students about different varieties of dinosaurs. The text uses digitally-modeled images and vivid photographs to explore a wide range of dinosaurs. Well-known species are included, along with lesser-known types, such as the Masiakasaurus. This is a unique text, sure to interest your animal lovers and dinosaur fans.

Fantastical Creatures and Magical Beasts
Shannon Knudsen
870L
ISBN: 978-0822599876

This 48-page book is a good mix of fantasy and informational text. While the topic of imaginary beasts usually leads to fictional reading, this text handles it differently. Readers learn the fictitious stories of numerous magical creatures, but learn the real story behind the myth. This is an excellent choice for students who enjoy fantasy. Rich colors, narrative-style writing, and succinct chapters make this a solid choice for many different types of readers.

Mummy Mysteries: Tales from North America
Brenda Z. Guiberson
1020L
ISBN: 978-0805053692

This entertaining text walks readers through a brief history of mummies. Organized like a chapter book, the text uses black-and-white photographs to show artifacts and mummies throughout. This text is excellent for exploring organizational features and physical text structures. Readers also have multiple opportunities to examine the relationships between sentences.

The Encyclopedia of Preserved People: Pickled, Frozen, and Mummified Corpses from Around the World
Natalie Jane Prior
1170L
ISBN: 978-0375822872

This text begins by explaining some of the differences between preserved bodies (mummies) and skeletons. This informational text presents basic facts and information in an engaging manner. Filled with images, illustrations, and full-color photographs, students can draw from multiple features to make meaning. There is a comprehensive index and bibliography included as well.

OUTER SPACE

International Space Station
Franklyn M. Branley
720L
ISBN: 978-0064452090

Readers learn about the functions on the International Space Station. This text is simple to understand, but provides a wealth of details and facts. This is also an *ALA Quick Pick* for reluctant readers.

Jupiter
Seymour Simon
820L
ISBN: 978-0064437592

This text is well-written and informative. Readers learn about Jupiter through rich photographs and detailed descriptions. The text is a great introduction to Jupiter and complimentary to many science units in these grades.

Moonshot
Brian Floca
990L
ISBN: 978-1416950462

This text traces the preparation for and the flight of Apollo 11 in 1969. The vivid colors and familiar picture-book style make this text an engaging and visually inviting choice for young readers. This is an appropriate choice for main ideas, details, connections, and summarizing.

Space Exploration
Carole Stott
1100L
ISBN: 978-0756658281

This reference book is broken into over twenty different two-page sections. With titles such as "How to be an Astronaut," "Danger and Disaster," and "Astronaut Fashion," each two-page spread is engaging and will easily ignite the curiosity of many students. Filled with full-color images and varied text features, this text is great for exploring this standard.

Team Moon: How 400,000 People Landed Apollo 11 on the Moon
Catherine Thimmesh
1060L
ISBN: 978-0618507573

This text explores the behind-the-scenes story of Apollo 11. Drawing from direct quotes and firsthand sources, Thimmesh tells of the challenges faced by the NASA staff and team responsible for the mission. The text features content-specific vocabulary, an index, and descriptions of the other Apollo flights. The white text printed on black paper makes the text visually appealing. Black-and-white photographs of the team, the space capsule, Buzz Aldrin, Neil Armstrong, and Michael Collins are included as well.

The Solar System
Laura Hamilton Waxman
650L
ISBN: 978-0761338741

This 48-page book is organized into six chapters. Chapters are typically less than ten pages long. Each page features vivid images and colorful, large print. An index, glossary, and suggested resources to learn more about the solar system are also included.

Thirteen Planets
David Aguilar
1120L
ISBN: 978-1426307706

This 64-page informational text is published by *National Geographic*. Organized as more of a reference book, this text discusses the redefinition of the word *planet*, explores the three dwarf planets, and explains about comets and asteroids. The images are stunning and vivid. Readers can explore multiple text structures and encounter a wide range of content-specific vocabulary.

Point of View

> *"If there is any one secret of success, it lies in the ability to get the other person's point of view and see things from that person's angle as well as from your own."*
>
> Henry Ford, *industrialist*

READING INFORMATIONAL TEXT STANDARD 6:
POINT OF VIEW

Third	Fourth	Fifth
Distinguish their own point of view from that of the author of a text.	Compare and contrast a firsthand and secondhand account of the same event or topic; describe the differences in focus and the information provided.	Analyze multiple accounts of the same event or topic, noting important similarities and differences in the point of view they represent.

GRADE LEVEL DIFFERENCES

Each grade level needs explicit instruction about point of view for this standard. *What is a point of view? How do we determine point of view?* Each grade level, however, will explore this differently. In the third grade, students just need to differentiate their viewpoints from that of the author. In the fourth grade, the students are looking at firsthand and secondhand sources. *What point of view do they provide? How are they different?* In the fifth grade, students are examining multiple accounts and evaluating the differences in point of view.

The *Point of View* standard is about **perspective.** Students are developing an awareness of how we situate our understanding of an issue or idea and the differences that exist.

Key Point

The focus of this standard is not on narration type. If the instructional focus stays on classification of narration style, students will miss the entire core of the standard.

136

Third Grade

Students are recognizing that the author has a point of view, while considering how it differs from their own viewpoint. This means that students are reading an informational text, making a decision about what viewpoint the author holds, and then forming their own viewpoint as a point of comparison. One misconception about this standard is that point of view focuses on narration style. This leads to lessons on first, second, and third person. While valuable, the focus of this standard is not on narration type. If the instructional focus stays on classification of narration style, students will miss the entire core of the standard. This standard is about the author's perspective. *What does the author think or believe? What is the author's position?* Analysis should be centered on the author and his or her views and stances. After students have done this, they are basically turning the lens on themselves and asking those exact same questions. Once this has been done, students describe the differences and similarities between these viewpoints.

Fourth Grade

In the fourth grade, students need the same explicit instruction that third graders have in terms of what a viewpoint is. Their instruction will be extended to not only look at viewpoint generically, but to look at how two specific types of viewpoints are estab-lished and differentiated. Fourth graders will consider firsthand and secondhand sources. This should not be reduced to classification of sources as one type or the other. This should still be an **interrogation and comparison** of how these two types of sources differ in their presentation of content and point of view. Just as third grade focused on comparing the student's view to the author's view, fourth graders will compare a secondhand account to a firsthand account and share how they are similar or different.

Fifth Grade

In the fifth grade, students will still need the initial understanding of what point of view is. This is the universal foundation for each grade level. The next step for fifth graders will be to look at multiple sources that explore the same topic to analyze how their points of view are different. On a higher level, students are effectively asking how the text is attempting to position them. *How do the two accounts of an event or topic differ? How are the accounts the same?* Students should be able to conceptualize that even though authors write about the same subject, there are always variances in their presentation, word choices, visuals, and information included. These different things all work in conjunction and help readers establish and recognize the author's point of view.

WARNING!

Many fifth graders may have missed instruction about firsthand and secondhand sources the year before. Fifth grade teachers may need to go back and introduce this aspect of the standard as well.

1 *"Today we will learn about point of view. Your point of view is how you see things. Everyone, even me, has a different point of view. Think about where you are sitting in the classroom right now; everyone has a different view of me. Some of you are looking directly at the front of me. Others can see more of a side view. Some of you may not be able to see certain parts of my face or body because of the angle you are sitting at or maybe a taller person is blocking part of your view. Because of our different places in the room, we have different viewpoints. This is the same for authors. They have a certain way that they see things and it can be very different from the way that you see things or your friends see things."* **Third and fifth grade teachers can skip to step four next.**

2 **Explain that there are two types of points of view.** Note: step two and three are only required for fourth grade students. *"There are two types of viewpoints: firsthand and secondhand. Firsthand means that you were right there. You saw it up close and personal. You saw it with your own two eyes. Can you guys think of some events that you have been a firsthand witness to?"* Solicit responses and discuss. Expect birthdays, arguments, movies, vacations, or holiday celebrations.

3 **Next, provide an example of a secondhand account.** *"Secondhand accounts are when you were not there. For example, I was not born during the American Revolution, but I can read about it, do a bit of research, and write a secondhand account of the battles. Was I there? No. Did I see any of the war? No. I learned my information from other sources. Can anyone think of a time in your life when you learned about something secondhand?"* Solicit responses and discuss.

4 **Create an anchor chart with the students like the one shown here.** *"There are a few questions that can help you think about the author's point of view and your own point of view."* Point out that these questions all ask the same thing, but use different words. These questions are just guides to help students think about point of view.

5 **Select an informational text to read out loud.** Try to use a short selection that has an obvious stance or opinion. *"As I read, think about our point of view questions that we just listed. When I finish, let's see if we can answer one about the author's point of view and about your own."*

6 **After you read the text, call on students to respond to any of the questions from the anchor chart.** If you have fourth grade students, also ask them if the account was from a firsthand or secondhand source.

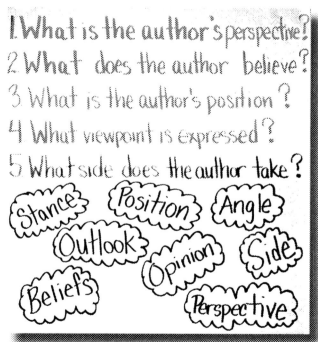

1. What is the author's perspective?
2. What does the author believe?
3. What is the author's position?
4. What viewpoint is expressed?
5. What side does the author take?

Stance   Position   Angle
Outlook   Opinion   Side
Beliefs   Perspective

Example of a Point of View anchor chart.

1   **Review the meaning of** *point of view* **and the difference between firsthand and secondhand viewpoints.** *"We talked about how your point of view is how you see things. This is your perspective. Everyone, including me, has a different point of view."*

2   **Select two informational text excerpts to share.** I think it is smart to select two texts with clearly opposite viewpoints. For fourth graders, you want to select both a secondhand and first-hand account.

Research Based

3   *"I want you to listen to both of these texts that I am going to read. Each expresses a different point of view. After we read, we will think back over the text and list similarities and differences between the viewpoints of each author."* Note: If you teach third grade, you will only need to read one text. Students should identify similarities and differences between their own points of view and that of the author.

"A major goal of the guided instruction phase in the gradual release of responsibility model is to create an environment for students where they can begin to apply what they are learning. Mastery is not the goal. The teacher is there to provide scaffolds to support and guide learners."

(Frey & Fisher, 2010, p. 85).

4   **As you read the text(s) to your students, stop to think out loud, wonder, question, and make predictions.** Some students will want to ask questions and interact. This is great; encourage this! You want to support the idea that reading is an intellectual endeavor of curiosity and questioning. This should not be a situation where your students are sitting in silence.

5   **After you have finished reading the text(s), create a T-chart that you can write on and model for the students.** Label one side of the T-chart "similarities (+)" and the other side "differences (-)." Think out loud and begin to list at least one similarity and one difference that you notice. Discuss differences between the viewpoints with students.

6   **Call on students to help you add more similarities and differences.** Gradually re-lease responsibility and encourage students to take ownership of the information that is added to the chart. Repeat as needed with a second set of short texts. This can continue over a series of days, and students can work in groups, collaborative pairs, or individually.

138

THE ORGANIZERS

After you have explicitly introduced and modeled how to apply the strategies of this standard to text, you want to provide students with an organizer that they can use to think about their own informational text reading. In order to make sure that students can independently understand and use the organizer, it is important to model how the specific organizer is used. Select a text and organizer of your choice. Complete the organizer with your students and post it as a model. Afterwards, students can independently use that same organizer multiple times to practice the skill with different informational texts. This can be done in pairs, groups, and independently.

The two books that I use with each organizer in this chapter are *Rosa* by Nikki Giovanni and *Rosa Parks: My Story* by Rosa Parks and Jim Haskins. These two books are used for each example for this standard for consistency and to offer the same books as points of comparison for teachers.

1 Read (or reread) at least the first six pages of *Rosa*. This is a fairly straightforward picture book. Read (or reread) one or two pages from *Rosa Parks: My Story*. If you don't have a copy of each book for your students, simply project the text or use a document camera so that students can follow along and read it. Discuss how these two books are very different. As you talk with your students, be sure to use the language of this standard. Think out loud and complete the organizer together.

2 Once you model by explicitly completing the organizer, your students will understand the connection between the standard and the organizer. You can provide blank copies of the organizer and allow students to select their own informational text, assign one from your class anthology, or select a title from the suggested book list within this chapter.

3 Students can complete an organizer when they read any informational text. This can be done as an assignment and can be repeated as many times as you want with any informational text that you choose. The sky is the limit! This allows for multiple opportunities to tailor the text to the student and maintain fidelity to the standard.

4 Once students have demonstrated mastery of the skill, don't stop using it. You want your readers to keep practicing. In the introduction of the book, I discussed the pitfalls of being a Checklist Teacher. Students need to keep perfecting their skill sets.

5 Reuse the same organizer, make it into an anchor chart, or post exemplars for students to reference later. You can add the organizer to a standards-based center, pair it with your school's reading incentive program, or use it daily as evidence of reading.

MULTIPLE ACCOUNTS

Be deliberate in pointing out that firsthand sources give a more extensive peek into the emotions and perceptions of the person. School teaches those in 6-8.

140

Topic: Rosa Parks

Multiple Accounts

Rosa Parks: My Story (firsthand)	Rosa By: Nikki Giovanni (secondhand)
• The Thoughts and emotions of Rosa Parks are on almost every page.	• You see beautiful pictures, but they are drawn or painted.
• You learn about what Rosa did after the bus boycott.	• Rosa is called Mrs. Parks.
• You learn about Rosa's husband and family.	• You learn about 'colored' only areas.
• You see real pictures of Rosa.	• You learn why November 13, 1956 is so important.

As you write, talk about your own vocabulary and writing choices. I started with "nice" and talked it through to "beautiful." Your students can benefit from just hearing your inner conversation when you make your own choices and think about words.

We noted what type of source each book was. This is not required for third and fifth grade, but it really is a helpful practice.

Multiple Accounts

Topic: _____

LET'S COMPARE

I always try to model two texts that are very different. These two choices were a picture book compared to a chapter book about Rosa Parks.

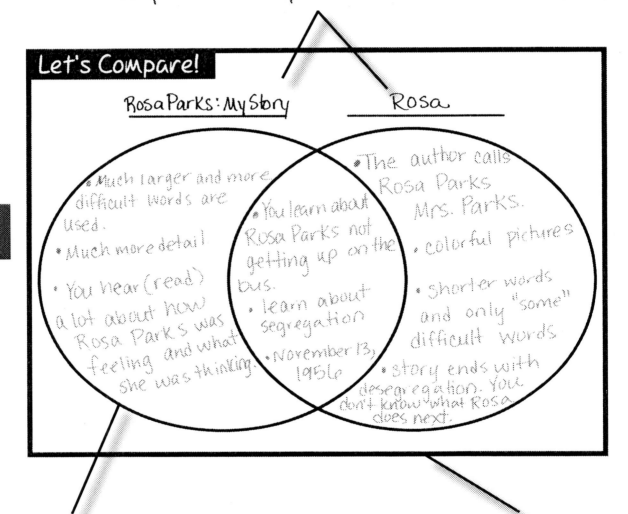

Let's Compare!

Rosa Parks: My Story | Rosa

* Much larger and more difficult words are used.
* Much more detail
* You hear (read) a lot about how Rosa Parks was feeling and what she was thinking.

* You learn about Rosa Parks not getting up on the bus.
* learn about segregation
* November 13, 1956

* The author calls Rosa Parks Mrs. Parks.
* colorful pictures
* shorter words and only "some" difficult words
* story ends with desegregation. You don't know what Rosa does next.

Remember that the standard for fourth graders is about looking at firsthand and a secondhand accounts.

This is also a great choice for an anchor chart. The simplicity lends itself to being recreated on larger chart paper or on an interactive whiteboard.

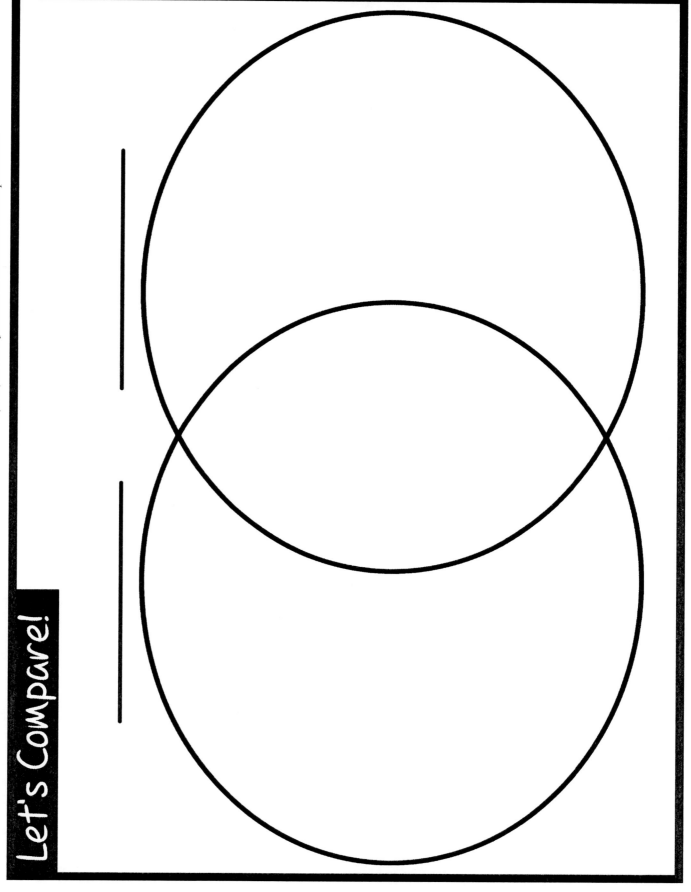

Let's Compare!

POINT OF VIEW CHART

Students can identify specific paragraphs, sections, topics, or parts of the text for this section. This is also an appropriate moment to revisit Standard 2: Main Idea.

This chart was created based on *Rosa* by Nikki Giovanni.

Topic / Ideas	Author's Point of View	My Point of View
Equality	Everyone should be treated fairly and have equal rights.	I think we should all be equal even if everyone looks different.
Hard Work	If you work hard, you can change the world.	You should work hard. It doesn't mean you will be the best, but you can try hard!!
Laws	Just because something is a law, doesn't make it fair or right.	I just think that laws are fair. Now I know that this is not always true.

Point of View Chart

This chart is a great match for third graders. The third-grade standard requires students to explain what point of view the author has and what their own viewpoint is.

Topic / Ideas	Author's Point of View	My Point of View

Point of View Chart

SIMILARITIES AND DIFFERENCES

An alternative is to have students use the language "compare/contrast" instead of "similarities and differences."

Similarities & Differences

	Similarities	Differences
Word Choice	Both books use historical words and the names of events are the same.	My story uses more difficult words. Rosa uses words that are more for kids.
Text Structure	Both books go in chronological (time sequence) order.	Rosa uses drawings. My story uses real photos from Rosa's life.
Ideas	Both books tell about Rosa Parks and her life.	My story tells more of Rosa's feelings and thoughts.

Note that the categories here are all based on informational text standards as well. This organizer is a great choice to use to reinforce multiple standards!

This organizer may require more scaffolding to help students combine learning from multiple standards into one thinking activity.

Similarities & Differences

Similarities

Differences

Word Choice

Text Structure

Ideas

Standard Six and Standard Nine both rely on students having access to more than one text about the same topic. As a result, this list is the **same** for both Standard Six and Nine. The exception to this is a list that I feature here, specifically for fourth-grade readers. The reason that fourth-grade readers have an additional text list here is because of the language of the standard. Standard Six: Point of View specifically states that fourth-grade students need to compare and contrast firsthand and secondhand accounts. Because of this demand, I have added a section called *Firsthand/Secondhand Accounts*. This list features book titles from a series (*In Their Own Words*) that integrate both types of accounts into one text. There are additional books on the suggested text list that are standalone firsthand sources as well. The books on the *Firsthand/Secondhand Accounts* list, however, are dedicated texts that include both types of point of view within one text.

FIRSTHAND/SECONDHAND ACCOUNTS

In Their Own Words

This Scholastic series, *In Their Own Words*, offers narrative-style biographies of historical figures, combined with images of firsthand sources from the subject. These inexpensive books would make a great addition to the library of any fourth-grade teacher. These are great choices to teach about firsthand and secondhand sources. Students get to differentiate, right in the same text, between sections that are firsthand accounts contrasted with the portions that are secondhand accounts (the narratives of the author's accompanying text). There are numerous subjects and topics included. Listed below are some of the titles/topics along with ISBN and Lexile® number. This is a great place to point out how the Lexile® of a book does not dictate grade-level usage. Remember that text complexity is based on reader task and qualitative measures for the majority of your instructional decisions. Consider how appropriate these texts are for the learning of this standard. Attention to the reader task is critical here.

- *Abraham Lincoln, 700L, ISBN: 978-0439147507*
- *Benjamin Franklin, 650L, ISBN:978-0439158060*
- *Betsy Ross, 690L, ISBN: 978-0439263214*
- *Christopher Columbus, 620L, ISBN: 978-0439158077*
- *Davy Crockett, 670L, ISBN: 978-0439263184*
- *Harriet Tubman, 660L, ISBN: 9780-439165846*
- *Helen Keller, 730L, ISBN: 978-0439147514*
- *Paul Revere, 740L, ISBN: 978-0439095525*
- *Pocahontas, 680L, ISBN: 978-0439165853*
- *Sitting Bull, 700L, ISBN: 978-0439263221*
- *Sojourner Truth, 690L, ISBN: 978-0439263238*
- *The Wright Brothers, 750L, ISBN: 978-0439263207*
- *Thomas Edison, 670L, 978-0439263191*

CHOCOLATE

Chocolate
Katie Daynes
760L
ISBN: 978-0794507596
This book uses easy-to-understand vocabulary and short sentences throughout. This is a good choice for struggling or reluctant readers. This 48-page text is filled with a wide variety of images and multiple text structures to help readers make meaning.

Chocolate: Riches from the Rainforest
Robert Burleigh
980L
ISBN: 978-0810957343
This colorful book includes captions, bold print, timelines, drawings, and photographs to detail the history of chocolate. Tracing the origins of chocolate historically, the text includes references to the Aztecs, slaves, rainforests, and the cacao tree. There is a good balance of serious, historical details and fun, modern facts. Readers get a bevy of fun information about Milton Hershey and even the Tootsie Roll factory.

How is Chocolate Made?
Angela Royston
700L
ISBN: 978-1403466419
This 32-page book walks readers through the process of making milk chocolate. The book is a great example of chronological/sequential order. The world maps, photographs, and colors will engage students from start to finish. This text works well with multiple age groups.

Smart About Chocolate: A Sweet History
Sandra Markle
730L
ISBN: 978-0448434803
This fun book is filled with colorful pages, photographs, drawings, and text. Most appropriate for third graders, this text has great examples of different text structure. Markle shares facts that can be integrated into writing, and presents a form of informational text that is packed with details and facts, yet remains engaging and entertaining.

The Story Behind Chocolate
Sean Price
730L
ISBN: 978-1432923471
Filled with interesting tidbits of information about chocolate, this book is sure to grab the interest of your curious fact finders. Readers learn how the Aztecs made chocolate, when chocolate-chip cookies were invented, and a slew of other lesser-known facts about chocolate. Rich photographs and text features are found throughout the text.

149

FOSSILS

A T. Rex Named Sue: Sue Hendrickson's Huge Discovery
Natalie Lunis
800L
ISBN: 978-1597162593
Readers explore with paleontologist Sue Hendrickson. Bright colors and photographs fill the pages of this text, which traces her digs in the badlands of South Dakota. Readers learn how she discovered the fossil remains of a T-Rex that later became known as Sue.

Dinosaur Detectives
Peter Chrisp
770L
ISBN: 978-0789473837
This book is equally balanced with text and images. The adventures of Jack Horner and Mary Anning are included as readers are introduced to paleontology. Rich photographs, drawings, and text features make this visually appealing. This is a great choice for your dinosaur and science lovers alike.

Fossils
Ann Squire
1010L
ISBN: 978-0516225043
This text guides readers through the different eras in fossil discovery, explains how fossils are created, and offers a suggested reading list. A variety of text features are found throughout the book. This book also contains a balance of content-specific vocabulary and conversational word choices.

How Does a Bone Become a Fossil?
Melissa Stewart
870L
ISBN: 978-1406211252
This text answers questions about bones. Readers learn how minerals collect on bones and the process that turns bones into fossils. This text explores multiple cause-and-effect relationships as well. At 32 pages long, this is a manageable text for young readers.

The Fossil Feud
Meish Goldish
710L
ISBN: 978-1597162562
This text recounts the "Bone Wars," a long-standing rivalry between two paleontologists. The text traces how the relationship turned sour in 1868 and the following two decades. As the rivalry unfolds, readers learn about extraordinary discoveries, dinosaur facts, and a wide variety of content-specific vocabulary.

LEWIS AND CLARK

Animals on the Trail with Lewis and Clark
Dorothy Hinshaw Patent
1090L
ISBN: 978-0395914151
This text is packed with photographs, varied text structures, maps, and illustrations. At over 120 pages, this book offers a great deal of information on a wide variety of animals often seen during the period of American expansion. Students are presented with such a variety of information and imagery, that engagement with this text is often very high. This book works well with each grade level to teach multiple standards.

Lewis and Clark
George Sullivan
710L
ISBN: 978-0439095532
This 128-page book uses firsthand documents to guide readers through the experiences of Captains William Clark and Meriwether Lewis. The narratives that explain the documents are engaging and keep students wondering what will happen next. Focusing mostly on illustrations and journal entries, the text is a great tool to demonstrate the differences between firsthand and secondhand sources.

PBS: Lewis and Clark
Ken Burns
http://www.pbs.org/lewisandclark/index.html
This digital resource offers multiple types of informational text and multimodal resources about Lewis and Clark. This site is appropriate to model what hyperlinks are and how to use them to navigate and find information. Students are able to read biographies of Lewis and Clark and the members of their Corps of Discovery. Readers can learn about the different groups of Native Americans, the historical context of the time, and navigate an interactive map of the trail that the explorers traveled. There are video and audio interviews and even multiple Q&A sessions with Ken Burns. Under a section titled *Archive* students can access additional websites about Lewis and Clark, a bibliography, and links to their personal journals. This offers an additional look at some firsthand and secondhand sources. Additionally, at the bottom of the site map, there are classroom resources and lesson plans for teachers.

MARS

Discovering Mars: The Amazing Story of the Red Planet
Melvin Berger
670L
ISBN: 978-0590452212
This is just one of 200 books written by this award-winning author. Crafted in his usual

style of hands-on activities and interesting facts, Berger's book is a great example of informational text. Students can identify connections in the text and easily make sense of the main ideas and details.

Mars: Distant Red Planet
David Jefferis
1000L
ISBN: 978-0778737322
The bright cover and rich images will interest students right away. Each page is filled with multiple captioned photographs and call-out boxes. Readers are presented with a wide variety of statistical data about Mars. Everything from the temperature to the distance from the Earth is presented in a reader-friendly format. This is also a great book for the Beyond Text standard.

Mission to Mars
Eve Hartman and Wendy Meshbesher
710L
ISBN: 978-1410939968
Organized into seven chapters, this book describes real-life missions to Mars, possible future colonies there, and the similarities between Mars and Earth. A glossary, timeline, and index are also included. A great balance of imagery and text make this book interesting, yet informative. As a bonus, readers are also provided with a great list of websites to visit to learn more about Mars.

NASA: Mars Exploration Program
http://mars.jpl.nasa.gov/allaboutmars/
This web page is part of a larger NASA website on Mars. This specific link features three different sections on Mars: "Mars Mystique," "Mars in the Night Sky," and "Mars: Extreme Planet." The navigation bar at the top also has a multimedia link which leads to a collection of images, interactive tools, and videos.

PIRATES

Pirate
Richard Platt
1150L
ISBN: 978-0679872559
This text is filled with images, colorful print, and photographs. The readers get to take an up-close look at the life of pirates. Readers learn about the Jolly Roger, what daily life was like, and tactics employed by pirates. This text is appropriate for multiple informational text standards.

Pirates and Smugglers
Moira Butterfield
1120L
ISBN: 978-0753462485
This 64-page book is organized into three chapters, with multiple subsections within each chapter. Each one chronologically takes readers through the history of piracy. Sections include titles such as "Female Pirates," "Pirates Today," and "Buccaneers." The text also offers readers a book list and set of websites to learn more about pirates and smugglers.

Pirateology
William Lubber
1180L
ISBN: 978-0763631437
This text is presented as the journal of an early eighteenth-century pirate hunter. The photographs and two-page spreads look like worn parchment. Readers visit China, the Caribbean, and Madagascar. Filled with a variety of text structures, this is an appropriate model to explore sidebars, visual imagery, and maps.

The History of Pirates
Allison Lassieur
800L
ISBN: 978-0736864237
This 32-page book shares a variety of historical facts about the Golden Age of Piracy. The controlled vocabulary and the short length of the text make this a comfortable choice for struggling readers. The illustrations are dramatic and beautiful, with photographs and prints throughout the text.

True Stories of Pirates
Lucy Lethbridge
1120L
ISBN: 978-0794508753
This 144-page text is organized around descriptive, engaging topics. Readers can learn about the Golden Age of Piracy, Captain Kidd, and the story of two young women pirates. Each of the stories is organized very much like fiction, but report a series of true events. This is a great transition for readers who are reluctant to move from literary text into informational text.

What If You Met a Pirate?
Jan Adkins
920L
ISBN: 978-1596430075
This fun informational text examines the myths surrounding pirates. The playful tone that Adkins is known for is carried throughout the text. The book is filled with interesting and little-known facts. The vivid color-washed pages use multiple text features to inform and help readers make meaning.

153

ROSA PARKS

Who Was Rosa Parks?
Yona Zeldis McDonough
700L
ISBN: 978-0448454429
This book is part of a larger series of student-friendly biographies that are readable for younger children. The books in this series are enjoyable for both very young children and older elementary students. These are great choices for modeling your own thinking in the classroom. They provide basic content about Rosa Parks' life, challenges, and accomplishments through narrative dialogue, well-written text, and varied illustrations.

Rosa
Nikki Giovanni
900L
ISBN: 978-0312376024
This book is really much more than a biography of Rosa Parks. The text follows her early life as a seamstress and her famous refusal to forfeit her bus seat. This text puts the events of her life in context by outlining other key events of the era that help readers make sense of this time period. Readers learn about the pivotal Brown v. Board of Education decision, the Women's Political Caucus, Emmett Till, and Martin Luther King. The rich content is woven into the colorful and almost poetic language that can only come from Giovanni. Beautiful illustrations fill the book and balance the words with stunning visual imagery.

Rosa Parks: My Story
Rosa Parks and Jim Haskins
970L
ISBN: 978-0141301204
This autobiography features narrative vignettes about the childhood, marriage, and political participation of Rosa Parks. She shares her own stories and references numerous figures from the Civil Rights era that she knew and worked with. She candidly addresses misconceptions and historical distortions of some events as well. This is an excellent example of a firsthand account.

SHARKS

Adventures of the Shark Lady: Eugenie Clark Around the World
Ann McGovern
890L
ISBN: 978-0590457125
McGovern is a storyteller at heart. Her biography follows the life and adventures of Eugenie Clark. Readers learn about her experiences as a marine biologist known for diving with great white sharks. Readers also discover facts about sharks, crabs, and a variety of other sea creatures. The descriptions are detailed and sensory.

The Life Cycle of a Shark
John Crossingham
930L
ISBN: 978-0778706694

Readers learn about the life cycles of sharks through full-color photographs, bold words, a glossary, and an index. Each of the fifteen chapters is filled with detailed information and presented in an easy-to-understand, two-page-or-less format. Chapters are much more like sections rather than longer, more traditional chapters. This is a great choice to introduce readers to the concept of informational text chapter books.

Shark
Meish Goldish
900L
ISBN: 978-1597169424

This 24-page book is organized into nine chapters. There are online resources, a reading list, bibliography, glossary, and index included. Colorful photographs are found throughout the book and offer up-close images of a variety of sharks. This engaging text can be used to support the instruction of multiple standards.

Shark-a-Phobia
Grace Norwich
930L
ISBN: 978-0545317825

Bright blues and greens fill the pages of this informational text. Readers learn about where to find sharks, how to protect themselves, and finally ways to overcome any fear of sharks. The text structures are obvious and somewhat playful. Words are written in a variety of colors, with a glossary of terms and definitions throughout.

Sharks
Penelope Arlon
900L
ISBN: 978-0545495615

This text is organized into short, mostly two-page sections. Readers learn about a variety of sharks such as the Hammerhead, Mako, and Horn Shark. Full-color photographs include intriguing close-ups. The captions are plentiful and informative throughout.

Sharks (Scary Creatures)
Penny Clarke and Mark Bergin
900L
ISBN: 978-0531146729

This text relies on a question-and-answer format to teach about the nutritional needs, environment, and body systems of the shark. Readers take a look at the internal workings of sharks through colorful images, bullets, captions, and text. A glossary, index, and chapter names are included.

155

Women's Suffrage

Elizabeth Leads the Way: Elizabeth Cady Stanton and the Right to Vote
Tanya Lee Stone
700L
ISBN: 978-0312602369
Watercolor illustrations fill each page of this text. The author uses rhetorical questions and a conversational tone to explain Stanton's experiences and contributions to the women's suffrage movement. Readers will enjoy the picture-book style and feel of the text.

Great Women of the Suffrage Movement
Dana Meachen Rau
950L
ISBN: 978-0756512705
This collection of biographies chronicles the lives of well-known and lesser-known figures in the women's suffrage movement. Readers are introduced to seven influential women including Susan B. Anthony, Alice Paul, and Ida B. Wells. Black-and-white photographs compliment the well-written text.

You Want the Women to Vote, Lizzie Stanton?
Jean Fritz
870L
ISBN: 978-0698117648
This biography of American feminist Elizabeth Cady Stanton is an empowering read. Fritz uses her lively voice to bring to life the events of Stanton's life. Crafted with a variety of sentence structures and content-specific vocabulary, this text is informative, yet engaging.

You Wouldn't Want to Be a Suffragist!
Fiona MacDonald
830L
ISBN: 978-0531207017
This text is a part of the *History of the World* series created by David Salariya. The book explains the concepts of equal rights and women's suffrage. Most of the text focuses on the hardships and consequences of being an advocate for women's rights during that time period. At 32 pages, this text is a brief but lucid introduction to the topic. Readers can look for connections between individuals, events, and ideas.

Women's Right to Vote
Terry Collins
740L
ISBN: 978-1429623414
This hard-to-find text explains the women's suffrage movement in a graphic-novel format. Readers are able to learn the facts of the movement, but enjoy the feel of a comic. Vivid colors and drawings are throughout the text. This is a great compliment to some of the more traditionally-formatted texts on this topic.

Women's Right to Vote (Cornerstones of Freedom Second Series)
Elaine Landau
900L
ISBN: 978-0531188330
Despite being only 48 pages long, this text is filled with facts and details. Sentence variety and content-specific vocabulary fill each page. Readers learn about the first public convention on women's rights, inequality, and the struggle to transform the voting system. A glossary of terms such as *radical, temperance movement, prejudice,* and *valiant,* followed by a timeline, complete this text.

WRIGHT BROTHERS

Can You Fly High, Wright Brothers?
Melvin Berger and Gilda Berger
720L
ISBN: 978-0439833783
This text combines interesting facts about the Wright brothers' early lives with a wealth of information about the more well-known events in their lives. Filled with vivid illustrations, photographs, and wonderful text features, this text is engaging for students in all grades.

First Flight: The Story of the Wright Brothers
Leslie Garrett
900L
ISBN: 978-0789492913
This informational text is filled with photographs, sidebars, captions, bold headings, and illustrations. The engaging feel of the text really makes this a good choice for a variety of readers. There are a great deal of facts and ideas that students can use to make connections and summarize.

Taking Flight: The Story of the Wright Brothers
Stephen Krensky
840L
ISBN: 978-0689812248
This is an excellent choice for struggling readers. The book is set up to resemble a chapter book, but is only 48 pages and has large type. This short biography is filled with a variety of text structures and vivid watercolor illustrations. Students can compare this with other books on the same topic or read it as a standalone text to examine structure, sequential order, or word choice.

157

To Fly
Wendie Old
780L
ISBN: 978-0618133475
This 48-page book is organized into 15 chapters and includes an epilogue, an index, and a suggested reading list. While watercolor images are included, this book is really much more about the text. The images are almost just decorative, with the content being fully woven into the words. Each chapter is less than three pages long. The varied sentence structures, length, and type make this appropriate for your higher readers as well.

Beyond Text

"The seeing of objects involves many sources of information beyond those meeting the eye when we look at an object."
Richard Gregory, *psychologist*

READING INFORMATIONAL TEXT STANDARD 7:
BEYOND TEXT

Third	Fourth	Fifth
Use information gained from illustrations (e.g., maps and photographs) and the words in a text to demonstrate understanding of the text (e.g., where, when, why, and how key events occur).	Interpret information presented visually, orally, or quantitatively (e.g., in charts, graphs, diagrams, time lines, animations, or interactive elements on Web pages) and explain how the information contributes to an understanding of the text in which it appears.	Draw on information from multiple print or digital sources, demonstrating the ability to locate an answer to a question quickly or to solve a problem efficiently.

GRADE LEVEL DIFFERENCES

Students in each grade level will interpret information from visual and digital sources. In third grade, students are simply tasked with using the information to demonstrate an understanding of the text. In the fourth grade, students are asked to explain how the information helps them make meaning. In practice, both of these look almost identical. In the fifth grade, students are expected to use information from multiple sources to answer questions or solve problems.

The *Beyond Text* standard is really about expanding the definition of text to reach beyond just the printed letter to include maps, photographs, charts, diagrams, interactive digital elements, and animations. The wording of this standard for each grade level is very different. Students in third grade are expected to use information gained from multimodal sources to demonstrate understanding of a text. Fourth graders are asked to explain how this information contributes to an understanding of a text. Fifth graders are asked to draw on information. To demonstrate mastery, each grade level still has two key foundational skills at their core:

- Interpret information from a variety of multimodal text.
- Understand how the information helps readers make meaning.

Students can demonstrate this core understanding in a variety of ways across each grade level, but they each need those two basic skills. As your students move from third through fifth grade there are specific emphases or steps that they are expected to take:

- The first step (3rd grade) is to use multimodal information to **answer questions** or demonstrate comprehension in other ways.
- The second step (4th grade) is to **interpret** the information and **explain** how it helps readers make meaning.
- The final step (5th grade) is to **rely on multiple sources** to answer questions or solve problems.

To explicitly teach this standard, teachers need to spend time exploring different types of "texts." Second, teachers need to help students verbalize the strengths and benefits commonly associated with different modalities. Finally, students need opportunities to gather information from different types of sources to answer questions and solve problems.

As teachers, we need to understand what different types of "texts" exist so that we can familiarize our students with these frequently. This list can be expansive because it includes everything that is not a traditional print sentence or paragraph. An effective practice is to teach students not just to read these multimodal elements, but to use them in their own writing as well. A fun idea is to regularly feature one type of "beyond text" structure as part of the opening or closing of your day. Ask students to represent their day or the night before in that format. For example, if you use illustration, ask them to tell about their day in a picture. If you are using a diagram, ask them to choose an aspect of their day to diagram. They might make a pie chart of what they did or a graph of activities that they enjoyed or disliked. Quick bell-ringers like these are good ways to reinforce this concept with students as readers and writers.

While this standard may appear to be an easier or lighter standard compared to others, it is one of the most relevant to the ways that students gather information today. This standard is one that has not been given a great deal of focus within traditional language and reading courses. With the constantly changing modes of communication and the abundance of audio, visual, and multimedia information available for consumption, this standard grows increasingly more relevant.

1 **Connect this standard to Standard Five: Text Structure.** *"When you read informational text, you rarely have just words. You have a lot of physical text structures. We talked about this when we learned about text structures earlier. Today we are going to talk more about how these structures can help readers answer questions about text."*

2 **Share with students that there are lots of ways to think about words.** *"When readers have an informational text, they look at the illustrations, charts, diagrams, and images to help them make sense of text. If the text is online, there can even be animations, graphics, and other information that helps answer questions."*

3 *"Let's talk about some common structures that we might see when we read an informational text."* Create an anchor chart (like the model on below). As you add a structure, show an example and ask students to discuss what questions this type of structure can help readers answer.

Common Core
Buzzword

Use the language of the standards when discussing vocabulary:

Interactive Elements

Charts

Graphs

Diagrams

Time Lines

Maps

Photographs

161

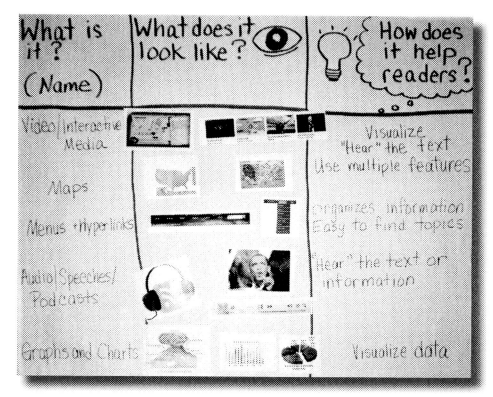

Anchor chart showing examples of different types of non-text features.

1 **Select an informational text that utilizes photographs, illustrations, and maps for your third graders.** For fourth and fifth, I like to use a digital news story or online text with lots of interactive features. See the suggested text list for some ideas. I try to use content that is engaging or at least somewhat familiar.

2 **Project the text so that all students have access to it.** Explain to students that you are looking for features *beyond* just sentences and paragraphs that help you make sense of the text.

3 **Read the text aloud.** When you encounter an illustration, map, photograph, chart, diagram, interactive digital feature, or timeline, stop and literally ask yourself, out loud, what the feature is and how it helps you understand the text. Add the feature to your list and verbalize how it provided information. This can become an anchor chart or can be written on the board.

4 **Review each of the features that you have recorded on the chart and ask students how it helped you make sense of the text.** *"Let's talk about the parts of this text that helped us understand it better."*

Beyond Text Standard

Feature ?	How does it help me to understand ?
First image of the volcano erupting. Lava is flowing. **Photograph**	Helps readers see how large, powerful, explosive, and scary a volcano is.
pahoehoe written in *italics*	Makes the word look different from the other words. It stands out.
aa (AH-ah) parentheses	Tells readers how to say/pronounce a word correctly
drawing of the ocean floor color-coding and arrows are used.	Shows the different areas under the sea. You can see the different sizes and names of the sections.

Key Point

There are a couple of variations to be conscious of. For your third graders, the standards seem to focus more on features that can exist entirely in print (as opposed to digital) text. For your fourth and fifth graders, digital features are specifically mentioned. An additional point of difference is that fifth graders don't just gather information for mastery of this standard. This grade level is tasked with **solving a problem** or **answering a question** through the features.

An analysis of text features found within Volcanoes *by Seymour Simon.*

THE ORGANIZERS

After you have explicitly introduced and modeled how to apply the strategies of this standard to text, you want to provide students with an organizer that they can use to think about their own informational text reading. In order to make sure that students can independently understand and use the organizer, it is important to model how the specific organizer is used. Select a text and organizer of your choice. Complete the organizer with your students and post it as a model. Afterwards, students can independently use that same organizer multiple times to practice the skill with different informational texts. This can be done in pairs, groups, and independently.

The book that I use with each organizer in this chapter is *A History of US: The First Americans: Prehistory–1600* by Joy Hakim. This book is used for each example for this standard for consistency and to offer the same book as a point of comparison for teachers.

1 Read (or reread) one to two pages from *A History of US: The First Americans: Prehistory–1600* to your students. If you don't have a copy for each student, project the text or use a document camera so that students can follow along and read it. As you talk with your students, be sure to use the language of this standard. Think out loud and complete the organizer together.

2 Once you model by explicitly completing the organizer, your students will understand the connection between the standard and the organizer. You can provide blank copies of the organizer and allow students to select their own informational text, assign one from your class anthology, or select a title from the suggested book list within this chapter.

3 Students can complete an organizer when they read any informational text. This can be done as an assignment and can be repeated as many times as you want with any informational text that you choose. The sky is the limit! This allows for multiple opportunities to tailor the text to the student and maintain fidelity to the standard.

4 Once students have demonstrated mastery of the skill, don't stop using it. You want your readers to keep practicing. In the introduction of the book, I discussed the pitfalls of being a Checklist Teacher. Students need to keep perfecting their skill sets.

5 Reuse the same organizer, make it into an anchor chart, or post exemplars for students to reference later. You can add the organizer to a standards-based center, pair it with your school's reading incentive program, or use it daily as evidence of reading.

ANSWERING QUESTIONS

I like to have students highlight or underline where they note content-specific vocabulary so that we can discuss the meaning in context.

The language of the standards asks fifth graders to use the information to answer questions. Third and fourth graders are not required to complete this additional step, but it is always good practice to begin thinking about this.

164

Answering Questions		
Source / Feature	Information Included	What Questions Does This Answer?
Map showing <u>conquistadors</u> routes	The sequential order that the explorers traveled.	Where did the explorers go?
Image of a horse being lifted on a ship.	A drawing with a horse held up in the air to <u>hoist</u> it onto the ship.	How did explorers travel once they reached land? How did horses get onboard when there was no gangplank?
Yellow <u>callout</u> box on pg. 121	(barbacoa) Defines barbecue and uses it with its original meaning.	What is a barbacoa?

When using this organizer with fifth graders, this column should represent multiple SOURCES. For third and fourth graders this section represents multiple FEATURES within one text.

Answering Questions

Source / Feature	Information Included	What Questions Does This Answer?

QUESTIONING THE TEXT

Students enjoy noticing how the non-text features mirror the text or expand on it to help it make more sense.

This organizer works well with third and fourth graders. It would be more appropriate for fifth graders to use one organizer for each source.

we noted when information from both illustrations and text was exactly the same.

Questioning the Text		
My Questions	From Words	From Illustrations
What types of foods did the explorers eat?	Corn (Called Maize)	Corn
Did explorers have animals onboard?	Horses were only hoisted onto the ship when they couldn't get closer.	A horse is pulled by rope onto a ship.
Where did Spanish explorers travel to?	From the Atlantic ocean to the Pacific ocean. ⟵—SAME	From the Atlantic to the Pacific ⟶
What is a griffin?	This is a mythical (not real) animal that explorers thought was real.	This looks like a bird and cat mixed together.

I like to do a picture-walk first with the students. This is a great way to generate questions. Once we record the questions in the "My Questions column," we read on and note where we gathered information from.

Questioning the Text

My Questions	From Words	From Illustrations

CHARTING INFORMATION

I really like to use this when students have a complex feature or one that provides a lot of information. Let them unpack what information is included and think about how that helps readers.

Although it seems counter-intuitive, working from the source down to the question (last) really gets the students to consider how this information is helpful.

Charting Information

Source / Feature

> Map of the different routes that the Spanish explorers traveled.

⬇

Information Included

> A map of the country with a red arrow showing the order that they followed when the traveled.

⬇

What Question Does This Answer?

> where did the explorers go?

This is a great organizer to use when considering digital sources. Students can really deconstruct how the various features work to help readers.

Charting Information

Source / Feature	Information Included	What Question Does This Answer?

UNDERSTANDING THE TEXT

This organizer can be cut in half so that students can examine text features individually.

This is a simple organizer, but just right for introducing this skill. It gives a clear picture of how to "read" non-text features.

Understanding the Text

Feature

The map on page 123 showing the route of the explorers.

Feature

The image of the lance on page 126.

How Does This Help Me Understand the Text?

I can see where the explorers went. It helps me wonder more about why they went that way and what happened.

How Does This Help Me Understand the Text?

I can picture what a lance looks like and know what authors mean when they write about one.

Note that I really have more questions than answers about the text here. That is okay! Remember that questioning as you read is part of making sense of text and a key part of comprehension and thinking!

170

Understanding the Text

Feature

How Does This Help Me
Understand the Text?

Feature

How Does This Help Me
Understand the Text?

The categories used to group the titles on this list are very narrowly focused. For example, instead of a category called "Explorers," there is a specific category for Lewis and Clark. This is a response to the learning embedded within the standard. For third and fourth grade, this standard centers on your students' ability to use visual information from a text (digital or print) to make meaning. Each text listed includes multiple photographs, diagrams, or interactive elements. Any of the books on this list would be appropriate for this standard.

Fifth-grade students, however, are expected to draw from multiple sources to learn about a specific subject, not just use multiple visual elements from text. Each category here includes at least one print book and one digital source to meet that need. This allows your fifth graders to use all of the titles listed under a category in conjunction to gather information. A student could easily select one of the categories as their subject of exploration and draw from all of the sources there to meet the rigor of this standard. You, or your students, could also easily create your own subject lists. The lists here could simply serve as a model of how text types can be grouped to gather information. Your fifth graders may also benefit from the paired book lists included for Standard Six: Point of View and Standard Nine: Multiple Sources when practicing this standard.

COLONIAL LIFE

Colonial Life
Brendan January
770L
ISBN: 978-0516271941
January explains the farming, medicine, and food of colonial life. Readers learn about the branches of government and important American symbols. The glossary, word list, and index help readers to navigate the text and understand content-specific words and concepts.

Colonial Life
Bobbie Kalman
870L
ISBN: 978-0865055117
Readers learn about the early homes and communities of the colonists. Readers learn what their daily lives were like, what children did for fun, and how people traveled. Kalman also briefly explains the hardships of plantation life for slaves. This 32-page long book is a clear, succinct overview of colonial life.

History Channel: Thirteen Colonies

http://www.history.com/topics/thirteen-colonies

This website houses a collection of digital resources about the colonies. Rich articles about each colony and the different types of colonies are available. At the time of publication, there were fifteen different videos available. Each video is less than four minutes long and is of the same quality you would find on the History Channel. Also included are 17 different photo galleries, organized by colony names and figures from the era.

The Dreadful, Smelly Colonies

Elizabeth Raum

810L

ISBN: 978-1429663519

This text explores the difficulties of life in the thirteen colonies. Readers learn why colonists had to resort to a wide-range of practices that we would consider dangerous and unsanitary today. This book is a great match for both your history buff and lover of all things gross.

The Real Story About Government and Politics in Colonial America

Kristine Carlson Asselin

720L

ISBN: 978-1429672191

This text explores the difficult life of the colonial era. Instead of whitewashing the period, the text tackles some of the strange things that went on in the colonies. Students learn about morbid medical practices, as well as the use of whippings as punishments. The text focuses on the strains of British rule and the eventual fight for independence. The book also includes a wide range of illustrations and paintings.

The Scoop on Clothes, Homes, and Daily Life in Colonial America

Elizabeth Raum

780L

ISBN: 978-1429672139

This 32-page book is a great companion to other books on colonial life. Readers learn how colonists dressed and the daily challenges that they faced. Written in plain language, this text still includes content-specific vocabulary throughout.

The Scoop on School and Work in Colonial America

Bonnie Hinman

790L

ISBN: 978-1429679862

This straightforward book creates a clear and easy-to-understand image of colonial daily life. This is a great text for students to critically contrast their own experiences in school to those of the colonists. This 32-page book is a great overview of this topic.

173

EVOLUTION

PBS: Evolution

http://www.pbs.org/wgbh/evolution/

This is a huge database of videos, articles, images, and materials for teachers about this topic. While a controversial subject in many places, it is highly comprehensive for the Beyond Text standard. It may be useful to visit the website and select specific links that meet the needs of your classroom.

Billions of Years, Amazing Changes: The Story of Evolution

Laurence Pringle

1000L

ISBN: 978-1590787236

This 112-page book examines evidence from genetics, paleontology, and geology to make an argument for evolution. Readers have multiple opportunities to examine main ideas, details, evidence, and reasons. A comprehensive glossary is included, along with an index, drawings, full-color photographs, and a recommended reading list.

What Is the Theory of Evolution?

Robert Walker

1100L

ISBN: 978-0778772057

Written by an investigative reporter, this 64-page text examines the evidence that supports and explains this theory. This text is a great companion to science classes that study evolution. This is also appropriate when evaluating evidence and reasons. As always, carefully consider the composition of your classroom along with district and school expectations when considering a text in support of or opposition to evolution.

LEWIS AND CLARK

Animals on the Trail with Lewis and Clark

Dorothy Hinshaw Patent

1090L

ISBN: 978-0395914151

This text is packed with photographs, varied text structures, maps, and illustrations. At over 120 pages, this book offers a great deal of information on a wide variety of animals often seen during the period of American expansion. Students are presented with such a variety of information and imagery, that engagement with this text is often very high. This book works well with each grade level to teach multiple standards.

How We Crossed the West: The Adventures of Lewis and Clark

Rosalyn Schanzer

890L

ISBN: 978-0792267263

This 48-page book is filled with a wealth of details and information about the experiences of Lewis and Clark. This text was written from the diaries of Lewis and Clark. The author uses excerpts to unfold the narrative of their explorations. Rich illustrations help bring the story alive for readers.

Lewis and Clark
George Sullivan
710L
ISBN: 978-0439095532
This 128-page book uses firsthand documents to guide readers through the experiences of Captains William Clark and Meriwether Lewis. The narratives that explain the documents are engaging and keep students wondering what will happen next. Focusing mostly on illustrations and journal entries, the text is a great tool to demonstrate the differences between firsthand and secondhand sources.

PBS: Lewis and Clark
Ken Burns
http://www.pbs.org/lewisandclark/index.html
This digital resource offers multiple informational text and multimodal resources on Lewis and Clark. This site is appropriate to model what hyperlinks are and how to use them to navigate and find information. Students are able to read biographies of Lewis, Clark, and the members of their Corps of Discovery. Readers can learn about the different groups of Native Americans, the historical context of the time, and navigate an interactive map of the trail that the explorers traveled. There are video and audio interviews and even multiple Q&A sessions with Ken Burns. Under a section titled *Archive* students can access additional websites about Lewis and Clark, a bibliography, and links to their journals. This offers an additional look at some firsthand and secondhand sources. Additionally, at the bottom of the site map, there are classroom resources and lesson plans for teachers.

MUMMIES

Thirteen Creepiest Mummies on Earth
Environmental Graffiti
http://www.environmentalgraffiti.com/news-creepiest-mummies?image=0
This slide show features thirteen images of mummies, with a paragraph to accompany each. The photographs are engaging and the paragraphs have a wide variety of sentence structures and varying sentence lengths. Each photograph also has a hyperlink to the author of the text, the source of the image, or the photographer.

Mummies: A Strange Science Book
Sylvia Funston
1070L
ISBN: 978-1894379045
Readers learn what qualifies as a mummy, and how they actually become mummified. Readers learn about famous mummies that have been found in Egypt, as well as lesser-known locations where mummies have been found such as China and England. Colorful illustrations and photographs are found throughout the text as well.

Mummies of the Pharaohs
Melvin and Gilda Berger
1000L
ISBN: 978-0439335959

Written in the informative, yet accessible style that the Bergers are known for, this text is packed with information. Readers are introduced to King Tut, Ramses II, and a wide variety of other well-known and lesser-known Egyptian mummies. There are large, colorful photographs found on almost every page. This 64-page book comes in hardcover and paperback; the paperback version is often difficult to locate, but both editions have the same information.

Mummy Mysteries: Tales from North America
Brenda Z. Guiberson
1020L
ISBN: 978-0805053692

This entertaining text walks readers through a brief history of mummies. Organized like a chapter book, the text uses black-and-white photographs to show artifacts and mummies throughout. This text is excellent for exploring organizational features and physical text structures. Readers also have multiple opportunities to examine the relationships between sentences.

Smithsonian: Egyptian Mummies
http://www.si.edu/Encyclopedia_SI/nmnh/mummies.htm

This is a more difficult text with almost an overload of content-specific words and challenging vocabulary. This is an appropriate choice for your fifth graders who need a challenging text or are above grade level, but interested in this topic. This offers those students a great balance with the other lower-level texts.

BOG BODIES

Archaeological Institute of America: Bodies of the Bogs
http://archive.archaeology.org/online/features/bog/

This website includes an article on peat bog preservation. At the end of the text, there are multiple hyperlinks to explore different facets of "bog people." Students can read about the restoration process, and view photographs of mummies and bog people.

Bodies from the Bog
James Deem
1100L
ISBN: 978-0395857847

The author introduces readers to the story of Danish workmen who were digging in a peat bog and discovered a dead body. The body was fully preserved. In the text, readers follow scientists as they examine him and explain who he is and how his body was preserved by the peat bog.

Bog Bodies
Natalie Jane Prior
1110L
ISBN: 978-1864482430

This 96-page book explores a wide variety of mummies and human corpses. The images will be sure to excite and delight your readers who enjoy the gross and creepy! The author explains what a "bog body" is and how it is preserved. Full-color photographs appear throughout the text.

WALT DISNEY

Biography.com: Walt Disney
http://www.biography.com/people/walt-disney-9275533

This website includes biographical information about Disney and his creations. There are three biographical video clips and footage of his theme parks.

The Story of Walt Disney
Bernice Selden
870L
ISBN: 978-0440402404

Organized into ten chapters, this text reads like a novel. Each chapter is about ten pages long and includes a wide variety of information about Walt Disney's life and the characters that he is so famous for creating.

Walt Disney, Graphic Biography
Saddleback Educational Group
760L
ISBN: 978-1599052304

This book is an engaging choice for this age group. Each colorful page is organized to look like a vividly-colored comic book. Speech bubbles and nontraditional fonts help tell the story of Disney's life and contribution to entertainment.

Who Was Walt Disney?
Whitney Stewart
720L
ISBN: 978-0448450520

Students learn about the early, small-town life of Walt Disney. This 112-page book is organized into chapters with names like "A Fantasy World" and "Final Act." Black-and-white images, a bibliography, and timelines are included.

177

Evidence & Connections

"Everything is connected . . . no one thing can change by itself."

Paul Hawken, *author*

Reading Informational Text Standard 8:
EVIDENCE & CONNECTIONS

Third	Fourth	Fifth
Describe the logical connection between particular sentences and paragraphs in a text (e.g., comparison, cause/effect, first/second/third in a sequence).	Explain how an author uses reasons and evidence to support particular points in a text.	Explain how an author uses reasons and evidence to support particular points in a text, identifying which reasons and evidence supports which point(s).

Grade Level Differences

This standard is the most varied across grade levels. In the third grade, students are looking for connections. This practice is virtually identical to what fourth and fifth graders focus on in Standard Five: Text Structure. Third graders are looking at the way that sentences and paragraphs are organized to show these structures. They focus on how sentences and paragraphs are connected in terms of structure. In the fourth and fifth grade, students focus on evidence and support for arguments: *What reasons support the author's claims? How does the evidence support specific points in the text?*

The *Evidence and Connections* standard focuses on looking at specific excerpts of text through a writer's lens. Readers are actually looking at the structure of sentences and paragraphs to determine how they are connected. Be careful not to confuse this with Standard Five: Text Structure. In third grade the standard specifically references cause/effect and comparison. This is the same language used in the other grade levels for the Text Structure standard. Let's take a moment and differentiate between those two standards. Standard five is about the **overall structure** of a text. Standard eight is about looking at **specific** sections, paragraphs, and sentences to determine what role they play. *How are those two sentences related? How does one support or explain the other?*

✎ Writing Connection

The skills of this standard are the same skills that students will use when writing their own arguments. In fact, the very same informational texts that students read for this standard can become mentor texts to consider when they write.

Third Grade

In the third grade, students are just expected to look at two sentences or paragraphs and see if they can find a **connection.** Students are examining the relationship between sentences. *How does sentence one help sentence two? Which sentence explains what happened first? Second? Third? Which sentence helps to make a comparison? A contrast? Which sentence shows the cause? The effect?* These are the connections that third graders are looking for. Be careful to focus on the sentences and paragraphs, not on the organizational pattern of the entire text.

Fourth and Fifth Grade

The standards for fourth and fifth grade are much more explicit about the type of connection that students are looking for. They are looking for **reasons, evidence, and support for a larger topic sentence.**

While third graders have a fairly general task, fourth and fifth graders really have to think like a writer. *What point is the author making? Which specific evidence helps to support that point?* To get started, students need to be able to find an argument, then determine how that argument is supported. For fourth and fifth graders, this standard also directly ties in with argument writing. The skill set required to evaluate evidence is the same one required when teaching students to write their own arguments. When students craft these arguments, they need to make claims and support them with valid reasons and evidence. For the Evidence & Connections standard, students are asked to look at another piece of writing and assess what the author did. While this is a reading standard, teachers need to consider the structure and information needed for writing. The same introduction and modeling used here can also be used to introduce argument writing. In fact, the very same informational texts that students read can become mentor texts to consider for their own writing organization.

It is important to notice that this standard is about looking specifically at informational text that makes a claim, asks the reader to take action, or is persuasive in nature. While I believe that everything is an argument, narrative nonfiction is probably not the best choice for the introduction of this standard. When you plan for explicit instruction, you want to select pieces that give the most clearly articulated examples of what you want to model. News articles, magazines, and commentary pieces are well-suited to offer students multiple ways to interrogate text and look for evidence. The suggested text list includes options that meet these criteria.

1 **To prepare for this lesson, type up several paragraphs where you state an opinion or make a claim.** Be sure to use at least an 18-point font and include lots of supporting evidence. This is a great time to be a bit silly or write about topics particularly relevant to your students. Cut each of the sentences apart. You should end up with a set of sentences that need to be put back in order. An alternative is to do the same thing, but use large sentence strips instead.

2 **Explain to your students that they will work as detectives today.** I enjoy showing an image of Sherlock Holmes or Encyclopedia Brown and dressing up as a detective. This is a fun day to bring in a magnifying glass, deerstalker hat, and patterned cape. If you can find them at your local party store, give out some toy magnifying glasses to the class. *"Today we will be detectives. We are investigating how sentences are related. These sentences are a bit like people in our investigation. We want to investigate what these people know about each other and how they work together."*

3 *"We have several sentences that are connected in some way, but we have to figure out how they are connected. Let me share with you what I know so that you can help."* Create an anchor chart like the one shown here.

4 **Pass out the mixed-up paragraphs to your students.** *"Here are the suspects that we are investigating. As detectives, I want you to determine how they work together."*

5 **Ask students to put the sentences in order and to think about their connections.** Note: third graders need to look for compare/contrast, sequential order, and cause/effect. Fourth and fifth graders are looking for the main topic and the reasons.

6 **Repeat with the different paragraphs.** Call on different "detectives" to share what they have found.

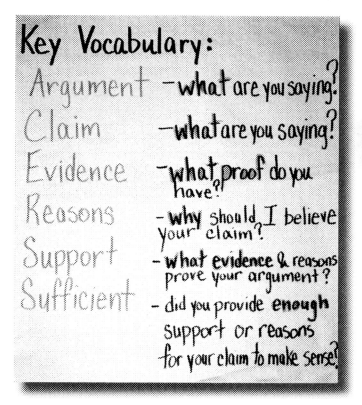

Key Vocabulary:
Argument — what are you saying?
Claim — what are you saying?
Evidence — what proof do you have?
Reasons — why should I believe your claim?
Support — what evidence & reasons prove your argument?
Sufficient — did you provide enough support or reasons for your claim to make sense?

Example of an anchor chart for Evidence and Connections.

181

1 **Remind students of their previous discussion about being detectives.** *"Today we will continue to work as detectives. We are still investigating how sentences are related. The last time we talked about this skill, you all had a lot of sentences that were all mixed up. Today I want to share with you how I investigate and think about relationships between sentences when I read. You might find some strategies that you can borrow when you are reading like a detective."*

2 **Share an informational text paragraph with your class (make a copy for each student).** For third graders look for a choice that relies on compare and contrast, sequential order, and cause and effect. For fourth and fifth graders select a piece that proposes an argument or makes a claim.

3 **Read the text out loud.** As you read, ask students to underline each sentence in a different color or alternating colors. Explain that, as detectives, we are thinking about how these sentences are all related.

4 **Refer back to the anchor chart about sentence relationships (in the *Introduce* section).** Read each one out loud. I like to wonder aloud after I read each one. *"Did I notice any of those connections? Hmm…"*

5 **Select two sentences.** I usually go directly for one that shows the argument and one that supplies the reason or evidence (fourth and fifth grade), or the first or second step in a sequence.

6 **Write one sentence, explaining which type of relationship you noticed from the anchor chart.** Repeat this as many times as necessary within the same passage or by pulling from multiple paragraphs. A great resource for this is your social studies text or the leveled readers that often come with these types of book series. They frequently feature cause and effect, sequential events, and arguments. If you pull examples from your social studies book, make sure that you use content that students have already learned rather than new content for this lesson.

7 **Be sure to include as many students in this process of looking for relationships as you can.** Call on different "detectives" to share relationships that they find. When they do find a sentence relationship, have them explain that relationship, in a complete sentence that uses the language of the standards.

THE ORGANIZERS

After you have explicitly introduced and modeled how to apply the strategies of this standard to text, you want to provide students with an organizer that they can use to think about their own informational text reading. In order to make sure that students can independently understand and use the organizer, it is important to model how the specific organizer is used. Select a text and organizer of your choice. Complete the organizer with your students and post it as a model. Afterwards, students can independently use that same organizer multiple times to practice the skill with different informational texts. This can be done in pairs, groups, and independently.

The book that I use with each organizer in this chapter is *Volcanoes* by Seymour Simon. This book is used for each example for this standard for consistency and to offer the same book as a point of comparison for teachers.

1 Read (or reread) *Volcanoes* to your students. I really like to use a text that students have read or are familiar with. If you shared *Volcanoes* when you modeled a different standard, that is fine, and in many cases preferable. If you don't have a copy for each student, project the text or use a document camera so that students can follow along and read it. As you talk with your students, be sure to use the language of this standard. Think out loud and complete the organizer together.

2 Once you model by explicitly completing the organizer, your students will understand the connection between the standard and the organizer. You can provide blank copies of the organizer and allow students to select their own informational text, assign one from your class anthology, or select a title from the suggested book list within this chapter.

3 Students can complete an organizer when they read any informational text. This can be done as an assignment and can be repeated as many times as you want with any informational text that you choose. The sky is the limit! This allows for multiple opportunities to tailor the text to the student and maintain fidelity to the standard.

4 Once students have demonstrated mastery of the skill, don't stop using it. You want your readers to keep practicing. In the introduction of the book, I discussed the pitfalls of being a Checklist Teacher. Students need to keep perfecting their skill sets.

5 Reuse the same organizer, make it into an anchor chart, or post exemplars for students to reference later. You can add the organizer to a standards-based center, pair it with your school's reading incentive program, or use it daily as evidence of reading.

183

CLAIMS & EVIDENCE

This organizer is specific to the standard for fourth and fifth graders. These two grade levels are looking specifically for reasons and evidence to support claims.

I like to have students determine if a sentence supports a claim as a reason or evidence.

Claims & Evidence

Claim / Point: **Hawaiian lava is thin and flows quickly.** → Reasons / (Evidence:) • **Speeds as high as 35 miles per hour have been measured.**

Claim / Point: **The eruption of Mount St. Helens was the most destructive in the history of the United States.** → Reasons / (Evidence:) • **Sixty people lost their lives.** • **Hundreds of houses and cabins were destroyed.**

Claim / Point: **Volcanoes don't just happen any place.** → (Reasons) Evidence: **Almost all volcanoes happen / erupt in places where two plates meet.**

It is a great practice to underline or highlight content-specific vocabulary words.

Claims & Evidence

Claim /
Point:

Reasons /
Evidence:

Claim /
Point:

Reasons /
Evidence:

Claim /
Point:

Reasons /
Evidence:

CONNECTING SENTENCES

This organizer works well with third graders and the requirements of the standard.

Sentence 1:   Pg #**16**

Hawaiian volcanoes erupt much more gently than did Surtsey or Mount St. Helens.

Sentence 2:   Pg #**16**

Only rarely does a Hawaiian volcano throw out rock and high clouds of ash.

How are these sentences connected?

☒ They compare things   ☐ They show a sequence (first, second, third)

☐ They show cause and effect

Explain your connection. How do you know?

The first sentence shows that the author is comparing Hawaiian volcanoes to Surtsey. The second sentence shows how Hawaiian volcanoes don't gush up and throw rock like Surtsey.

Connecting Sentences

186

Common Core
Buzzword
Get students in the habit of using the language of the standard when identifying connections.

Note how all standards connect back to Standard One: Textual Evidence. Students should get into the habit of supporting inferences and ideas about text.

Sentence 1:   Pg #

Sentence 2:   Pg #

How are these sentences connected?

☐ They compare things   ☐ They show a sequence
                                     (first, second, third)

          ☐ They show cause and effect

Explain your connection. How do you know?

Connecting Sentences

ARGUMENT PYRAMID

This is one of my favorite organizers to use with students. They have lots of space to write each sentence and get a visual of how the evidence and reasons support the author's point.

Argument Pyramid

Author's Point

The eruption of Mount St. Helens was the most destructive in the history of the United States.

Evidence / Reason #1

Sixty people lost their lives as hot gases, rocks, and ashes covered an area of 200 miles.

Evidence / Reason #2

Miles of highway roads, and railways were badly damaged.

Evidence / Reason #3

The force of the eruption was so great that entire forests were blown down like rows of matchsticks.

Note the similarity of this standard to the Textual Evidence standard. Students are still deconstructing how authors support and explain their thinking.

Writing Connection

Students can use this same organizer to plan their own argument writing.

Argument Pyramid

Author's Point

Evidence / Reason #1

Evidence / Reason #2

Evidence / Reason #3

THINKING ABOUT CONNECTIONS

Note that students can make multiple connections. They may notice cause/effect, sequence, or compare/contrast relationships throughout a paragraph or set of sentences.

Thinking About Connections

Sentence / Paragraph

Thick, slow-moving lava called aa (AH-ah) hardens into a rough tangle of sharp rocks.

Sentence / Paragraph

Thin, hot, quick-moving lava called pahoehoe (pah-HO-ee-ho-ee) forms a smooth, billowy surface.

How do these two help each other?
How are these two CONNECTED?

These sentences help you make a comparison. You can see how the two types of lava make different types of rock.

• Each sentence also shows an effect. The hot lava makes a new hard surface.
• That effect is also a similarity between them.

190

This graphic organizer is designed for the third-grade standard. Students need to determine how sentences are related.

Content-specific or challenging vocabulary is always underlined or highlighted. These make great words to discuss and add to the word wall.

Thinking About Connections

Sentence / Paragraph

Sentence / Paragraph

How do these two help each other?
How are these two CONNECTED?

BIOGRAPHIES/ MEMOIRS

Buried Alive! How 33 Miners Survived 69 Days Deep Under the Chilean Desert
Elaine Scott
1060L
ISBN: 978-0547707785

This text chronicles the story of the 33 miners that were trapped under the Chilean desert in 2010. Readers learn of the dangers associated with mining. A suggested reading list, glossary, and a wide variety of firsthand stories are included. There are also strong themes of community and hope. Multiple standards can be supported by this text.

Can You Fly High, Wright Brothers?
Melvin Berger and Gilda Berger
720L
ISBN: 978-0439833783

This text combines interesting facts about the Wright brothers' early lives with a wealth of information about the more well-known events in their lives. Filled with vivid illustrations, photographs, and wonderful text features, this text is engaging for students in all grades.

Fighting for Equal Rights
Maryann N. Weidt
810L
ISBN: 978-1575051819

This text explores the life of Susan B. Anthony. The text discusses ideas of women's rights, abolition, and equality. It also features the diverse career choices of Anthony, as an activist, journalist, and educator. There are multiple opportunities for connections between ideas, events, and people.

Fifty Cents and a Dream: Young Booker T. Washington
Jabvari Asir
740L
ISBN: 978-0316086578

This is a touching picture biography of Washington's life. Readers get a peek at some of the early experiences that shaped his life. The watercolor images throughout are engaging and match the tone of the text well. This text is thought-provoking and encourages critical discussions about multiple other subjects.

192

Helen Keller

Leslie Garrett

890L

ISBN: 978-0756603397

This inspirational and factual 128-page text frames Keller as a crusader. Young readers enjoy the plethora of color photographs and the images of various artifacts throughout this text. There are sidebars, definitions, call-out boxes, and multiple text structures that help students make meaning of the events in Keller's life.

Life in the Ocean: The Story of Oceanographer Sylvia Earle

Claire Nivola

1170L

ISBN: 978-0374380687

Readers are introduced to Sylvia Earle's early life as she grows up on a farm in Paulsboro, New Jersey. Introspective moments are shared as Earle reflects on her journal writing and early musings. Readers follow Earle as her family moves to Clearwater, Florida and Earle falls in love with the beauty of the Gulf of Mexico. Readers learn of her experiences and the choices that led her to an eventual career as an oceanographer. Inspiring and relatable, this text is a great example of narrative nonfiction.

Steve Jobs: Think Differently

Patricia Lakin

940L

ISBN: 978-1442453937

Written by a former elementary school teacher, this biography profiles Jobs and his work at Apple and Pixar. Readers learn of his adoptive parents, early life, and inventions. Jobs is portrayed as a rule-breaker who turned his curiosity and creativity into an empire. At 192 pages, this is most appropriate for your stronger readers.

Steve Jobs & Steve Wozniak: Geek Heroes Who Put the Personal in Computers

Mike Venezia

940L

ISBN: 978-0531223512

This 32-page book is filled with cartoon-style drawings, black-and-white photographs, and colorful images. Readers learn about the pioneers behind the Apple brand. Multiple text features such as an index, glossary, captions, and sidebars are included throughout. This is most appropriate for your younger readers.

When I Was Your Age: Volumes I and II: Original Stories About Growing Up

Amy Ehrlich

930L

ISBN: 978-0763604073

This 200-page book is an anthology of stories about growing up. Written by a variety of famous writers such as Avi, Laurence Yep, Walter Dean Myers, and Joseph Bruchac, the text is really geared toward your fifth-grade students. Most of the stories are about 20 pages long and work well as stand-alone essays or can be read for contrast, similar themes, and even as writing exemplars. Always preview these vignettes carefully for content and appropriateness for your students.

Human Body

Eyes and Ears
Seymour Simon
890L
ISBN: 978-0060733025
Readers explore colorful images as they learn about the anatomy of the eye and ear. Rich details and examples are provided throughout the text to help readers understand how these organs work. This is an excellent text to support multiple standards.

The Brain
Seymour Simon
900L
ISBN: 978-0060877194
Simon details the nervous system and the brain. Readers learn how different parts function and how they impact our every movement. Vivid images and details are found throughout. Readers have multiple opportunities to look for connections and main ideas.

The Digestive System
Christine Taylor-Butler
730L
ISBN: 978-0531168578
Taylor-Butler breaks the components and functions of the digestive system into manageable "bites." Common problems and diseases associated with digestion are also explored. Readers will enjoy the sidebars, illustrations, and recommended reading lists. This is a good choice for your struggling reader who has an interest in the human body.

The Heart: Our Circulatory System
Seymour Simon
1030L
ISBN:978-0060877217
Simon uses rich images to explain the functions of the circulatory system. Computer-enhanced images help to paint a realistic picture of the system. A variety of sentence types and structures are used throughout.

Outer Space

Flying to the Moon
Michael Collins
1170L
ISBN: 978-0374423568
This autobiography is categorized in the *Outer Space* section because of the great amount of detail that Collins provides about his time in space. This is definitely an autobiography, but the narrative descriptions of life aboard a space craft are rich and specific. At 172 pages long, this is for readers who have or are developing stamina for longer texts.

Galaxies

Seymour Simon

1010L

ISBN: 978-0688109929

This book is written in the informative style that Simon has become known for. The book features deep colors and images that vividly complement the text. Readers learn about the Milky Way and different categories of galaxies. This text can be used with any informational text standard.

International Space Station

Franklyn M. Branley

720L

ISBN: 978-0064452090

Readers learn about the functions on the International Space Station. This text is simple to understand, but provides a wealth of details and facts. This is also an *ALA Quick Pick* for reluctant readers.

Jupiter

Seymour Simon

820L

ISBN: 978-0064437592

This text is well-written and informative. Readers learn about Jupiter through rich photographs and detailed descriptions. The text is a great introduction to Jupiter and complimentary to many science units in these grades.

Moonshot

Brian Floca

990L

ISBN: 978-1416950462

This text traces the preparation for and the flight of Apollo 11 in 1969. The vivid colors and familiar picture-book style make this text an engaging and visually inviting choice for young readers. This is an appropriate choice when exploring main ideas, details, connections, and summarizing.

Team Moon: How 400,000 People Landed Apollo 11 on the Moon

Catherine Thimmesh

1060L

ISBN: 978-0618507573

This text explores the behind-the-scenes story of Apollo 11. Drawing from direct quotes and firsthand sources, Thimmesh tells of the challenges faced by the NASA staff and team responsible for the mission. The text features content-specific vocabulary, an index, and descriptions of the other Apollo flights. The white text printed on black paper makes the text visually appealing. Black-and-white photographs of the team, the space capsule, Buzz Aldrin, Neil Armstrong, and Michael Collins are included as well.

Thirteen Planets

David Aguilar

1120L

ISBN: 978-1426307706

This 64-page informational text is published by *National Geographic*. Organized as more of a reference book, this text discusses the redefinition of the word *planet,* explores the three dwarf planets, and explains about comets and asteroids. The images are stunning and vivid. Readers can explore multiple text structures and encounter a wide range of content-specific vocabulary.

WEATHER

A Drop of Water
Walter Wick
870L
ISBN: 978-0590221979
This scientific book is appropriate for early readers. Students trace the evolution of a snowflake and drop of water throughout the water cycle. Students learn about evaporation and condensation through close-up photographs and a variety of informative text features. Students can actively practice summarizing and sequential order.

Can it Rain Cats and Dogs? Questions and Answers About Weather
Melvin Berger
710L
ISBN: 978-0439085731
Organized to provide answers to a series of questions about weather, this text is accessible for all readers. Bright colors and vivid photographs are found on virtually every page. The simple, but factual, writing style makes this a straightforward text. This is a great text to practice summarizing and to examine connections.

Getting to the Bottom of Global Warming
Terry Collins
780L
ISBN: 978-1429639729
This text is presented in a graphic-novel format. Readers follow the experiences of Isabel Soto. Soto learns about global warming and takes the reader along. The text explains numerous aspects of global warming in a clear, easy-to-understand format. At just 32 pages, this text presents a great deal of information.

Green Living
Lucia Raatma
900L
ISBN: 978-0756542450
This 64-page text explores the concept of green living. Readers learn about environmental protection in an easy-to-understand format. The author uses content-specific vocabulary to provide an overview of major issues and lifestyle choices associated with environmental protection efforts.

Scholastic Question & Answer: What Makes an Ocean Wave?
John Rice, Gilda Berger, and Melvin Berger
870L
ISBN: 978-0439148825

I find that this book is most engaging for third graders. Students are introduced to a simple question-and-answer format, but with the familiar feel of a picture book. A simple question is asked, followed by a series of facts, images, and text that respond to the question. This book is part of the Scholastic *Question & Answer* series. These science-centered books all focus on different topics, most filled with varied physical text features and images. There are multiple other books in this series that explore the solar system, whales, tornadoes, and butterflies.

Severe Storm and Blizzard Alert
Lynn Peppas
1050L
ISBN: 978-0778716051

Readers examine the impact of hail, wind, storms, and lightning in this 32-page book. Readers are exposed to content-specific vocabulary throughout this science text. Practical explanations of Doppler radar are balanced with more dramatic descriptions of the Blizzard of 1888.

WRITING

Guy-Write: What Every Guy Writer Needs to Know
Ralph Fletcher
950L
ISBN: 978-0805094046

Fletcher's book offers tips and advice to help boys find their "sweet spot" as writers. Fletcher, author of over 40 books, describes writing as powerful; he debunks the misconception that writing is boring or for nerds. This text is a great choice to examine main idea and details. Fletcher also uses vocabulary in ways that will engage and interest your readers.

How to Write Your Life Story
Ralph Fletcher
940L
ISBN: 978-0060507695

This how-to book teaches students how to craft the story of their lives. Fletcher walks students through the steps that he suggests for crafting effective autobiographies. This instructional book is an excellent example of explanatory text. Students can also use this content when they are working on the writing standards. There is a chapter where Fletcher discusses how to write about "hard stuff." He shares an experience where someone dies quite suddenly and violently. Preview this section carefully to assess appropriateness for your students.

Multiple Sources

"It all depends on how we look at things, and not how they are in themselves."
Carl Jung, *psychiatrist*

READING INFORMATIONAL TEXT STANDARD 9:
MULTIPLE SOURCES

Third	Fourth	Fifth
Compare and contrast the most important points and key details presented in two texts on the same topic.	Integrate information from two texts on the same topic in order to write or speak about the subject knowledgeably.	Integrate information from several texts on the same topic in order to write or speak about the subject knowledgeably.

GRADE LEVEL DIFFERENCES

Students in each grade level are expected to analyze two or more texts. The third-grade requirements simply ask students to compare or contrast points and details. In the fourth and fifth grade, students are expected to integrate information from multiple texts into a written or verbal summary of the text.

Key Point

Keep in mind that this standard is multifaceted; it really defies classification as just a reading standard. Students will need to read, write, think critically, and explain to meet the goals and rigor of the Multiple Sources standard.

The *Multiple Sources* standard requires students to examine two or more texts on the same topic. Students are expected to analyze how those sources present information. This includes an analysis of the content, presentation, and word choices. This standard is about using a critical eye to examine more than one source of information. The language of the standard details specific areas of focus for each grade level.

Third graders are looking specifically for similarities and differences between the points and details presented in each text. Ideally, your third graders would examine at least two different sources, digital or print, and begin to compare them. *How are they alike? How are they different? What nuances or shades of gray exist?* Each of the standards, so far, have required students to think critically about informational text with an explicit focus on different aspects of critical thinking. This standard, Multiple Sources, is about integrating those skills into one task. Students will consider multiple facets of a text when analyzing what they read. They will draw from each of the standards to compare and contrast multiple texts.

Fourth and fifth graders are also expected to consider multiple sources on the same topic. The goal here is not just to compare and contrast these texts. Students in these grade levels are expected to integrate the information from these sources to write or speak about the subject. To demonstrate mastery, students in the fourth and fifth grade will need to move beyond just answering questions. They need to engage in a discussion and/or write about that topic. This is just as much a writing and research standard as it is a reading standard at this point. As a teacher, you want to make sure that you teach students to look at two texts about one topic and determine what information they can extract from each text.

To find success here, students need to have explicit practice comparing ideas, individuals, and events as they are presented by different authors. To teach this standard you need a set of paired readings that explore the same topic or at least similar subject matter. This is also a standard where students' interests can help guide the topic selection. Self-selected topics are effective and will result in higher levels of student engagement with this standard. A specific person, event, or cause can be great topics to begin with. The suggested text list includes some choices to guide you, but be flexible and let your students explore topics that matter to them when they work independently on this standard.

As you develop your instructional plan it will be easy to get overwhelmed. Keep in mind that this standard is multifaceted; it really defies classification as just a reading standard. Students will need to read, write, think critically, and explain to meet the goals and rigor of the Multiple Sources standard.

1 *"Today we will talk about ways that writers use information from two texts to write about a topic. Why do you think that someone would want to use information from two or more sources? Why not just pick a source and just use that one?"* Lead students to the idea that you can explain information much more accurately and thoroughly when you rely on multiple sources.

2 **Set the task for the day.** *"Today we are going to learn exactly how to compare what two different texts say and how to use information from two sources."*

3 **Distribute paper towels, plastic knives, two slices of bread, and peanut butter and jelly (or just jelly, check for peanut allergies first) to the class.** It is important that everyone has their own materials to make a sandwich. I find that it is much more effective to scoop out the peanut butter and jelly into smaller plastic cups so that you have about 10 smaller containers of peanut butter and jelly rather than passing two big ones around. The time and distraction of sharing the containers alone makes for a very different experience. Be prepared!

4 *"Today you each are going to be my sources. Each of you is playing the part of a text. I am going to learn how to make a sandwich from each of you. You are going to explain how to do this, step by step."* Ask students to make the sandwich at their desk and then make a list of each step that they followed to create the sandwich. This will be a messy, happy, fifteen-minute period. After the sandwiches are made, I set a timer for about 5-10 minutes and ask students to list the steps that they followed.

5 **Make multiple columns on the board.** Call on students to explain how they made their sandwiches or call five or six students up and have them write their instructions on the board. Be clear that they cannot *add* anything; they can only share what they have written down.

6 **Once you have several sets of directions, explain that you are ready to compare these sources.** Discuss differences and similarities. With this activity, students are bound to have left out major steps. Each list will have something that another student may have left out. Point out that if you only relied on one source you would not have the best set of directions. In order to be effective and really know about a topic, you need to integrate information from each source. For third graders, this is the end of where they need to go for this standard.

7 **For your fourth and fifth graders, you want them to now use the information in the columns to write about how to make the sandwich.** As you do this, point out that this process is the same one that they will use when they gather information from multiple text sources.

1 **Before beginning this model lesson, select two short passages or excerpts about the same topic.** See the suggested text list for sets organized by topic. I like to use passages that can be read aloud together and average about a page in length. This can be challenging to locate, so reading an excerpt is a great alternative.

2 **Explain that you decided to do research on a specific topic.** *"I decided to do a little research on (your topic of choice). I want to show you how I compare information from different sources and integrate the information so that I can talk about my topic."*

3 **Share one text at a time.** As you read, stop and discuss with students. Be certain to think out loud about your wonderings, predictions, or areas of confusion. When you finish reading the first text, create a T-chart and write the name of the text at the top. *"Now I want to look back at the text and think about what I learned. Let's see if I can list some of the ideas, facts, or information that I have learned from reading this one text."* Begin your list, referring back to the text as often as possible. Invite students to help add to the list by sharing what they learned from this text. Create a bulleted or numbered list.

4 **Repeat this same activity with the second text and record the information on the other side of the T-chart.** *"Let's try this again with our second text. It is about the same topic, but it is a different text, by a different author."*

5 Collaboratively discuss the differences between each text, noting characteristics of each. Circle the points that you find most important, explaining your thinking to your students. Work together to create a new list with the most important information. Think out loud and ask for support from students to create this new list.

Standard 9: Multiple Sources

Jan Adkins (What if you met a pirate?)	David Platt {Pirates}
• Real pirates were not flashy dressers.	• Most movies about pirates are really inaccurate.
• Pirates rarely died in battle. They usually died of diseases.	• Pirates weren't fancy dressers.
• Pirates did not take baths because fresh water was hard to get at sea.	• A pirate is just a person who plunders at sea.

T-chart comparing two different books about pirates.

202

THE ORGANIZERS

After you have explicitly introduced and modeled how to apply the strategies of this standard to text, you want to provide students with an organizer that they can use to think about their own informational text reading. In order to make sure that students can independently understand and use the organizer, it is important to model how the specific organizer is used. Select a text and organizer of your choice. Complete the organizer with your students and post it as a model. Afterwards, students can independently use that same organizer multiple times to practice the skill with different informational texts. This can be done in pairs, groups, and independently.

Select at least two informational text choices on the same subject or topic. There are many choices on the suggested text list at the end of this chapter or you can read two selections from your own collection. I chose three books on colonial life to model this standard. The three books that I use in this chapter are *The Dreadful, Smelly Colonies* by Elizabeth Raum, *The Scoop on School and Work in Colonial America* by Bonnie Hinman, and *The Real Story About Government and Politics in Colonial America* by Kristine Carlson Asselin.

1 Read (or reread) the first few pages from each of these books with your students. I like to do a picture walk and carefully examine the table of contents, chapter names, and glossaries of each of these choices. If you don't have a copy of each book for your students, be sure to project the text or use a document camera so that students can follow along and read it. Compare and contrast your different books. As you talk with your students, be sure to use the language of this standard. Think out loud and complete the organizer together.

2 Once you model by explicitly completing the organizer, your students will understand the connection between the standard and the organizer. You can provide blank copies of the organizer and allow students to select their own informational text, assign one from your class anthology, or select a title from the suggested book list within this chapter.

3 Students can complete an organizer when they read any informational text. This can be done as an assignment and can be repeated as many times as you want with any informational text that you choose. The sky is the limit! This allows for multiple opportunities to tailor the text to the student and maintain fidelity to the standard.

4 Once students have demonstrated mastery of the skill, don't stop using it. You want your readers to keep practicing. In the introduction of the book, I discussed the pitfalls of being a Checklist Teacher. Students need to keep perfecting their skill sets.

5 Reuse the same organizer, make it into an anchor chart, or post exemplars for students to reference later. You can add the organizer to a standards-based center, pair it with your school's reading incentive program, or use it daily as evidence of reading.

INTEGRATING SEVERAL TEXTS

We used the author's names to identify the text. I like to do this instead of the title because it reminds students that we are looking at someone else's writing. Just like students are authors when they write for a purpose, so is the person who wrote what we are reading in class. As readers, we deconstruct and analyze text.

when you model this organizer, you may want to break it up into several different class periods or simply complete one text at a time.

My Topic: Colonial Life Hardships

Text 1: Elizabeth Raum	Text 2: Bonnie Hinman	Text 3: Kristine Asselin
•Most colonists did not have guns, so they could not hunt for food. •Slaves and indentured servants did most of the work. •Most colonists had to walk everywhere. Carriages were very rare in 1697.	•Boys and girls had different skills to learn at school. • The only book owned by most families was the Bible. Books were very expensive.	•Lying, cheating, and not going to church were crimes. •Many criminals were branded. This is when a letter is burned into your hand or arm.

On the back or on a separate sheet of paper. Write one paragraph explaining your topic. Use information from each of your selected texts to explain and inform about your topic.

Integrating Several Texts

204

Remember that fourth and fifth graders have to use the information to speak or write about their topics.

My Topic:

Text 1:

Text 2:

Text 3:

On the back or on a separate sheet of paper. Write one paragraph explaining your topic. Use information from each of your selected texts to explain and inform about your topic.

Integrating Several Texts

INTEGRATING TWO TEXTS

As you think aloud with students to model how to complete the organizers, discuss challenging or domain-specific vocabulary.

Don't forget opportunities to integrate lessons about usage or style. Students tend to retain information when they are introduced to it in context.

My Topic: Colonial Life

Raum's
Text 1: The Dreadful, Smelly Colonies

Asselin's
Text 2: The Real Story About Colonial America

• Hunting for food was very hard because most colonists had no guns.

• Colonists walked everywhere. Having a carriage was rare.

• Bathrooms were outside and were very smelly.

• Criminals were often branded for their crime.

• Most colonies were run by a governor (appointed by the King of England).

• Lying, cheating and not going to church were crimes.

On the back or on a separate sheet of paper. Write one paragraph explaining your topic. Use information from each of your selected texts to explain and inform about your topic.

Integrating Two Texts

206

This can become a note-taking template for students. Now they can integrate the ideas into one piece of written text about the topic.

My Topic:

Text 1:

Text 2:

On the back or on a separate sheet of paper. Write one paragraph explaining your topic. Use information from each of your selected texts to explain and inform about your topic.

Integrating Two Texts

MOST IMPORTANT DETAILS

I find that students need to see this modeled multiple times. It is a challenge to determine what details to include.

This can really be a great lesson in note-taking. Students learn to go through a text and pull out information. This has applications for multiple content areas.

Most Important Details

Text #1

The Dreadful, Smelly Colonies
By: Elizabeth Raum

Most Important Details:

— There were very few ways to travel. The colonists walked everywhere.

— Indentured servants and slaves did most of the labor.

— Native Americans helped the colonists survive the first year.

VS.

Text #2

The Real Story About Government & Politics in Colonial America
By: Kristine Asselin

Most Important Details:

—There were lots of things that were illegal in the colonies that are not illegal today.

— The governor of each colony was appointed.

— It was difficult for colonists to make any laws or rules.

— You could be branded if you committed a crime.

Short on copies? This is one of those organizers that you can just have students make at their desks. Fold a piece of paper in half and write the title of the books at the top. Students have transitioned to actual notes from the model.

The Common Core Guidebook, 3-5: Informational Text Lessons

Most Important Details

Text #1

Most Important Details:

_____

_____

_____

_____

_____

vs.

Text #2

Most Important Details:

_____

_____

_____

_____

_____

The suggested text list for this standard is identical to the suggested text list for Standard Six: Point of View. Books are grouped by very narrow topics and are meant to be read in conjunction with other books on that same topic. The language of Standard Six: Point of View indicates that students should distinguish points of view when reading texts on the same topic. Standard Nine: Multiple Sources asks students to integrate, compare, and contrast information from texts on similar topics. This means that both Standard Six and Standard Nine rely on students having access to text sets. While the teaching focus may vary, the text sets for these two standards is the same. Organized by topic, this list is duplicated for both Standards Six and Nine.

CHOCOLATE

Chocolate
Katie Daynes
760L
ISBN: 978-0794507596
This book uses easy-to-understand vocabulary and short sentences throughout. This is a good choice for struggling or reluctant readers. This 48-page text is filled with a wide variety of images and multiple text structures to help readers make meaning.

Chocolate: Riches from the Rainforest
Robert Burleigh
980L
ISBN: 978-0810957343
This colorful book includes captions, bold print, timelines, drawings, and photographs to detail the history of chocolate. Tracing the origins of chocolate historically, the text includes references to the Aztecs, slaves, rainforests, and the cacao tree. There is a good balance of serious, historical details and fun, modern facts. Readers get a bevy of fun information about Milton Hershey and even the Tootsie Roll factory.

How is Chocolate Made?
Angela Royston
700L
ISBN: 978-1403466419
This 32-page book walks readers through the process of making milk chocolate. The book is a great example of chronological/sequential order. The world maps, photographs, and colors will engage students from start to finish. This text works well with multiple age groups.

Smart About Chocolate: A Sweet History
Sandra Markle
730L
ISBN: 978-0448434803
This fun book is filled with colorful pages, photographs, drawings, and text. Most appropriate for third-grade students, this text has great examples of different text structure. Markle shares facts that can be integrated into writing, and presents a form of informational text that is packed with details and facts, yet engaging and entertaining.

The Story Behind Chocolate
Sean Price
730L
ISBN: 978-1432923471
Filled with interesting tidbits of information about chocolate, this book is sure to grab the interest of your curious fact finders. Readers learn how the Aztecs made chocolate, when chocolate-chip cookies were invented, and a slew of other lesser-known facts about chocolate. Rich photographs and text features are found throughout the text.

COLONIAL LIFE

African-Americans in the Thirteen Colonies
Deborah Kent
990L
ISBN: 978-0516200651
Kent's moving book shares the facts about a time period when African-Americans are rarely mentioned in most social studies textbooks. Readers learn how the first Africans came to the colonies and worked alongside Europeans. Kent shares the history of contributions made by these workers, the evolution of their roles in the colonies, and the eventual system of slavery that resulted. This book is poignant and informative.

Colonial Life
Bobbie Kalman
870L
ISBN: 978-6505511778
Readers learn about the early homes and communities of the colonists. Readers learn what their daily lives were like, what children did for fun, and how people traveled. Kalman also briefly explains the hardships of plantation life for slaves. This 32-page long book is a clear, succinct overview of colonial life.

The Dreadful, Smelly Colonies
Elizabeth Raum
810L
ISBN: 978-1429663519
This text explores the difficulties of life in the thirteen colonies. Readers learn why colonists had to resort to a wide range of practices that we would consider dangerous and unsanitary today. This book is a great match for both your history buff and lover of all things gross.

211

The Fourth of July Story
Alice Dalgliesh
790L
ISBN: 978-0689718762

This 32-page book explains the history of the United States in a narrative format. Students learn factual information in a tone that feels very much like a conversation with the author. Organized into chapters, the book also includes rich illustrations on virtually every page.

The Real Story About Government and Politics in Colonial America
Kristine Carlson Asselin
720L
ISBN: 978-1429672191

This text explores the difficult life of the colonial era. Instead of whitewashing the period, the text tackles some of the strange things that went on in the colonies. Students learn about morbid medical practices, as well as the use of whippings as punishments. The text focuses on the strains of British rule and the eventual fight for independence. The book also includes a wide range of illustrations and paintings.

The Scoop on Clothes, Homes, and Daily Life in Colonial America
Elizabeth Raum
780L
ISBN: 978-1429672139

This 32-page book is a great companion to other books on colonial life. Readers learn how colonists dressed and the daily challenges that they faced. Written in plain language, this text still includes content-specific vocabulary throughout.

The Scoop on School and Work in Colonial America
Bonnie Hinman
790L
ISBN: 978-1429679862

This straightforward book creates a clear and easy-to-understand image of colonial daily life. This is a great text for students to critically contrast their own experiences in school to those of the colonists. This 32-page book is a great overview of this topic.

FOSSILS

A T. Rex Named Sue: Sue Hendrickson's Huge Discovery
Natalie Lunis
800L
ISBN: 978-1597162593

Readers explore with paleontologist Sue Hendrickson. Bright colors and photographs fill the pages of this text, which traces her digs in the badlands of South Dakota. Readers learn how she discovered the fossil remains of a T-Rex that later became known as Sue.

Dinosaur Detectives
Peter Chrisp
770L
ISBN: 978-0789473837

This book is equally balanced with text and images. The adventures of Jack Horner and Mary Anning are included as readers are introduced to paleontology. Rich photographs, drawings, and text features make this visually appealing. This is a great choice for your dinosaur and science lovers alike.

Fossils
Ann Squire
1010L
ISBN: 978-0516225043

This text guides readers through the different eras in fossil discovery, explains how fossils are created, and offers a suggested reading list. A variety of text features are found throughout the book. This book also contains a balance of content-specific vocabulary and conversational word choices.

How Does a Bone Become a Fossil?
Melissa Stewart
870L
ISBN: 978-1406211252

This text answers questions about bones. Readers learn how minerals collect on bones and the process that turns bones into fossils. This text explores multiple cause-and-effect relationships as well. At 32 pages long, this is a manageable text for young readers.

The Fossil Feud
Meish Goldish
710L
ISBN: 978-1597162562

This text recounts the "Bone Wars," a long-standing rivalry between two paleontologists. The text traces how the relationship turned sour in 1868 and the following two decades. As the rivalry unfolds, readers learn about extraordinary discoveries, dinosaur facts, and a wide variety of content-specific vocabulary.

LEWIS AND CLARK

Animals on the Trail with Lewis and Clark
Dorothy Hinshaw Patent
1090L
ISBN: 978-0395914151

This text is packed with photographs, varied text structures, maps, and illustrations. At over 120 pages, this book offers a great deal of information on a wide variety of animals often seen during the period of American expansion. Students are presented with such a variety of in-

213

formation and imagery, that engagement with this text is often very high. This book works well with each grade level to teach multiple standards.

Lewis and Clark
George Sullivan
710L
ISBN: 978-0439095532
This 128-page book uses firsthand documents to guide readers through the experiences of Captains William Clark and Meriwether Lewis. The narratives that explain the documents are engaging and keep students wondering what will happen next. Focusing mostly on illustrations and journal entries, the text is a great tool to demonstrate the differences between firsthand and secondhand sources.

PBS: Lewis and Clark
Ken Burns
http://www.pbs.org/lewisandclark/index.html
This digital resource offers multiple types of informational text and multimodal resources about Lewis and Clark. This site is appropriate to model what hyperlinks are and how to use them to navigate and find information. Students are able to read biographies of Lewis and Clark and the members of their Corps of Discovery. Readers can learn about the different groups of Native Americans, the historical context of the time, and navigate an interactive map of the trail that the explorers traveled. There are video and audio interviews and even multiple Q&A sessions with Ken Burns. Under a section titled *Archive* students can access additional websites about Lewis and Clark, a bibliography, and links to their personal journals. This offers an additional look at some firsthand and secondhand sources. Additionally, at the bottom of the site map, there are classroom resources and lesson plans for teachers.

MARS

Discovering Mars: The Amazing Story of the Red Planet
Melvin Berger
670L
ISBN: 978-0590452212
This is just one of 200 books written by this award-winning author. Crafted in his usual style of hands-on activities and interesting facts, Berger's book is a great example of informational text. Students can identify connections in the text and easily make sense of the main ideas and details.

Mars: Distant Red Planet
David Jefferis
1000L
ISBN: 978-0778737322
The bright cover and rich images will interest students right away. Each page is filled with

multiple captioned photographs and call-out boxes. Readers are presented with a wide variety of statistical data about Mars. Everything from the temperature to the distance from the Earth is presented in a reader-friendly format.

Mission to Mars
Eve Hartman and Wendy Meshbesher
710L
ISBN: 978-1410939968
Organized into seven chapters, this book describes real-life missions to Mars, possible future colonies there, and the similarities between Mars and Earth. A glossary, timeline, and index are also included. A great balance of imagery and text make this book interesting, yet informative. As a bonus, readers are also provided with a great list of websites to visit to learn more about Mars.

NASA: Mars Exploration Program
http://mars.jpl.nasa.gov/allaboutmars/
This web page is part of a larger NASA website on Mars. This specific link features three different sections on Mars: "Mars Mystique," "Mars in the Night Sky," and "Mars: Extreme Planet." The navigation bar at the top also has a multimedia link which leads to a collection of images, interactive tools, and videos.

PIRATES

Pirate
Richard Platt
1150L
ISBN: 978-0679872559
This text is filled with images, colorful print, and photographs. The readers get to take an up-close look at the life of pirates. Readers learn about the Jolly Roger, what daily life was like, and tactics employed by pirates. This text is appropriate for multiple informational text standards.

Pirates and Smugglers
Moira Butterfield
1120L
ISBN: 978-0753462485
This 64-page book is organized into three chapters, with multiple subsections within each chapter. Each one chronologically takes readers through the history of piracy. Sections include titles such as "Female Pirates," "Pirates Today," and "Buccaneers." The text also offers readers a book list and set of websites to learn more about pirates and smugglers.

215

Pirateology
William Lubber
1180L
ISBN: 978-0763631437
This text is presented as the journal of an early eighteenth-century pirate hunter. The photographs and two-page spreads look like worn parchment. Readers visit China, the Caribbean, and Madagascar. Filled with a variety of text structures, this is an appropriate model to explore sidebars, visual imagery, and maps.

The History of Pirates
Allison Lassieur
800L
ISBN: 978-0736864237
This 32-page book shares a variety of historical facts about the Golden Age of Piracy. The controlled vocabulary and the short length of the text make this a comfortable choice for struggling readers. The illustrations are dramatic and beautiful, with photographs and prints throughout the text.

True Stories of Pirates
Lucy Lethbridge
1120L
ISBN: 978-0794508753
This 144-page text is organized around descriptive, engaging topics. Readers can learn about the Golden Age of Piracy, Captain Kidd, and the story of two young women pirates. Each of the stories is organized very much like fiction, but report a series of true events. This is a great transition for readers who are reluctant to move from literary text into informational text.

What If You Met a Pirate?
Jan Adkins
920L
ISBN: 978-1596430075
This fun informational text examines the myths surrounding pirates. The playful tone that Adkins is known for is carried throughout the text. The book is filled with interesting and little-known facts. The vivid color-washed pages use multiple text features to inform and help readers make meaning.

ROSA PARKS

Who Was Rosa Parks?
Yona Zeldis McDonough
700L
ISBN: 978-0448454429
This book is part of a larger series of student-friendly biographies that are readable for younger children. The books in this series are enjoyable for both very young children and

older elementary students. These are great choices for modeling your own thinking in the classroom. They provide basic content about Rosa Parks' life, challenges, and accomplishments through narrative dialogue, well-written text, and varied illustrations.

Rosa
Nikki Giovanni
900L
ISBN: 978-0312376024

This book is really much more than a biography of Rosa Parks. The text follows her early life as a seamstress and her famous refusal to forfeit her bus seat. This text puts the events of her life in context by outlining other key events of the era that help readers make sense of this time period. Readers learn about the pivotal Brown v. Board of Education decision, the Women's Political Caucus, Emmett Till, and Martin Luther King. The rich content is woven into the colorful and almost poetic language that can only come from Giovanni. Beautiful illustrations fill the book and balance the words with stunning visual imagery.

Rosa Parks: My Story
Rosa Parks and Jim Haskins
970L
ISBN: 978-0141301204

This autobiography features narrative vignettes about the childhood, marriage, and political participation of Rosa Parks. She shares her own stories and references numerous figures from the Civil Rights era that she knew and worked with. She candidly addresses misconceptions and historical distortions of some events as well. This is an excellent example of a firsthand account.

SHARKS

Adventures of the Shark Lady: Eugenie Clark Around the World
Ann McGovern
890L
ISBN: 978-0590457125

McGovern is a storyteller at heart. Her biography follows the life and adventures of Eugenie Clark. Readers learn about her experiences as a marine biologist known for diving with great white sharks. Readers also discover facts about sharks, crabs, and a variety of other sea creatures. The descriptions are detailed and sensory.

The Life Cycle of a Shark
John Crossingham
930L
ISBN: 978-0778706694

Readers learn about the life cycles of sharks through full-color photographs, bold words, a glossary, and an index. Each of the fifteen chapters is filled with detailed information and presented in an easy-to-understand, two-page-or-less format. Chapters are much more like sections rather than longer, more traditional chapters. This is a great choice to introduce readers to the concept of informational text chapter books.

217

Shark
Meish Goldish
900L
ISBN: 978-1597169424
This 24-page book is organized into nine chapters. There are online resources, a reading list, bibliography, glossary, and index included. Colorful photographs are found throughout the book and offer up-close images of a variety of sharks. This engaging text can be used to support the instruction of multiple standards.

Shark-a-Phobia
Grace Norwich
930L
ISBN: 978-0545317825
Bright blues and greens fill the pages of this informational text. Readers learn about where to find sharks, how to protect themselves, and finally ways to overcome any fear of sharks. The text structures are obvious and somewhat playful. Words are written in a variety of colors, with a glossary of terms and definitions throughout.

Sharks
Penelope Arlon
900L
ISBN: 978-0545495615
This text is organized into short, mostly two-page sections. Readers learn about a variety of sharks such as the Hammerhead, Mako, and Horn Shark. Full-color photographs include intriguing close-ups. The captions are plentiful and informative throughout. .

Sharks (Scary Creatures)
Penny Clarke and Mark Bergin
900L
ISBN: 978-0531146729
This text relies on a question-and-answer format to teach about the nutritional needs, environment, and body systems of the shark. Readers take a look at the internal workings of sharks through colorful images, bullets, captions, and text. A glossary, index, and chapter names are included.

WOMEN'S SUFFRAGE

Elizabeth Leads the Way: Elizabeth Cady Stanton and the Right to Vote
Tanya Lee Stone
700L
ISBN: 978-0312602369
Watercolor illustrations fill each page of this text. The author uses rhetorical questions and a conversational tone to explain Stanton's experiences and contributions to the women's suffrage movement. Readers will enjoy the picture-book style and feel of the text.

Great Women of the Suffrage Movement

Dana Meachen Rau

950L

ISBN: 978-0756512705

This collection of biographies chronicles the lives of well-known and lesser-known figures in the women's suffrage movement. Readers are introduced to seven influential women including Susan B. Anthony, Alice Paul, and Ida B. Wells. Black-and-white photographs compliment the well-written text.

You Want the Women to Vote, Lizzie Stanton?

Jean Fritz

870L

ISBN: 978-0698117648

This biography of American feminist Elizabeth Cady Stanton is an empowering read. Fritz uses her lively voice to bring to life the events of Stanton's life. Crafted with a variety of sentence structures and content-specific vocabulary, this text is informative, yet engaging.

You Wouldn't Want to Be a Suffragist!

Fiona MacDonald

830L

ISBN: 978-0531207017

This text is a part of the *History of the World* series created by David Salariya. The book explains the concepts of equal rights and women's suffrage. Most of the text focuses on the hardships and consequences of being an advocate for women's rights during that time period. At 32 pages, this text is a brief but lucid introduction to the topic. Readers can look for connections between individuals, events, and ideas.

Women's Right to Vote

Terry Collins

740L

ISBN: 978-1429623414

This hard-to-find text explains the women's suffrage movement in a graphic-novel format. Readers are able to learn the facts of the movement, but enjoy the feel of a comic. Vivid colors and drawings are throughout the text. This is a great compliment to some of the more traditionally-formatted texts on this topic.

Women's Right to Vote (Cornerstones of Freedom Second Series)

Elaine Landau

900L

ISBN: 978-0531188330

Despite being only 48 pages long, this text is filled with facts and details. Sentence variety and content-specific vocabulary fill each page. Readers learn about the first public convention on women's rights, inequality, and the struggle to transform the voting system. A glossary of terms such as *radical, temperance movement, prejudice,* and *valiant,* followed by a timeline, complete this text.

WRIGHT BROTHERS

Can You Fly High, Wright Brothers?
Melvin Berger and Gilda Berger
720L
ISBN: 978-0439833783
This text combines interesting facts about the Wright brothers' early lives with a wealth of information about the more well-known events in their lives. Filled with vivid illustrations, photographs, and wonderful text features, this text is engaging for students in all grades.

First Flight: The Story of the Wright Brothers
Leslie Garrett
900L
ISBN: 978-0789492913
This informational text is filled with photographs, sidebars, captions, bold headings, and illustrations. The engaging feel of the text really makes this a good choice for a variety of readers. There are a great deal of facts and ideas that students can use to make connections and summarize.

Taking Flight: The Story of the Wright Brothers
Stephen Krensky
840L
ISBN: 978-0689812248
This is an excellent choice for struggling readers. The book is set up to resemble a chapter book, but is only 48 pages long and has large type. This short biography is filled with a variety of text structures and vivid watercolor illustrations. Students can compare this with other books on the same topic or read it as a standalone text to examine structure, sequential order, or word choice.

To Fly
Wendie Old
780L
ISBN: 978-0618133475
This 48-page book is organized into 15 chapters and includes an epilogue, an index, and a suggested reading list. While watercolor images are included, this book is really much more about the text. The images are almost just decorative, with the content being fully woven into the words. Each chapter is less than three pages long. The varied sentence structures, length, and type make this appropriate for your higher-level readers as well.

220

Akhondi, M., Aziz Malayeri, F., & Samad, A. A. (2011). How to teach expository text structure to facilitate reading comprehension. *The Reading Teacher, 64*(5), 368–372.

Almasi, J. F., & Fullerton, S. K. (2012). *Teaching strategic processes in reading.* New York: Guilford.

Anderson, R. C. (1984). Role of reader's schema in comprehension, learning and memory. In R. Anderson, J. Osborne, and R. Tierney (Eds.), *Learning to read in American schools.* Hillsdale, NJ: Lawrence Erlbaum Associates.

Anderson, R. C. (1995). *Research foundations for wide reading.* Urbana, IL: Center for the Study of Reading, Special Invitational Conference.

Baumann, J. F., Jones, L. A., & Seifert-Kessell, N. (1993). Using think-alouds to enhance children's comprehension monitoring abilities. *The Reading Teacher, 47*(3), 184-193.

Beers, K. (2003). *When kids can't read: What teachers can do.* Portsmouth, NH: Heinemann.

Caldwell, K., & Gaine, T. (2000). 'The Phantom Tollbooth' and how the independent reading of good books improves students' reading performance. San Rafael, CA: Reading and Communication Skills Clearinghouse. (ERIC Document Reproduction Service No. ED449462).

Duke, N. K., Pearson, P. D., Strachan, S. L., & Billman, A. K. (2011). Essential elements of fostering and teaching reading comprehension. In S. Samuels and A. Farstrup, *What research has to say about reading instruction* (pp. 94-114). Newark, DE: International Reading Association.

Fisher, D.. & Frey, N. (2007). *Checking for understanding: Formative assessment techniques for your classroom.* Alexandria, VA: Association for Supervision & Curriculum Development (ASCD).

Frey, N., & Fisher, D. (2010). Identifying instructional moves during guided learning. *The Reading Teacher, 64*(2), 84–95.

Frayer, D., Frederick, W. C., & Klausmeier, H. J. (1969). *A schema for testing the level of cognitive mastery.* Madison, WI: Wisconsin Center for Education Research.

Gallagher, K. (2004). *Deeper reading: Comprehending challenging texts.* Portland, ME: Stenhouse.

Gee, J. (2004). *Situated language and learning: A critique of traditional schooling.* New York: Routledge.

Harvey, S., & Goudvis, A. (2000). *Strategies that work: Teaching comprehension to enhance understanding.* Portland, ME: Stenhouse.

221

Hinchman, K. A., & Sheridan-Thomas, H. (2008). *Best practices in adolescent literacy instruction (solving problems in the teaching of literacy).* New York: The Guilford Press.

Mandel Morrow, L., & Gambrell, L. B. (2011). *Best practices in literacy instruction* (4th ed.). New York: The Guilford Press.

National Governors Association Center for Best Practices and Council of Chief State School Officers. (2010). *Common Core state standards.* Retrieved May 4, 2012 from http://www.corestandards.org.

National Institute of Child Health and Human Development. (2000). *Report of the National Reading Panel: Teaching children to read, an evidence-based assessment of the scientific research literature on reading and its implications for reading instruction.* Washington, DC: U.S. Government Printing Office.

Oster, L. (2001). Using the think-aloud for reading instruction. *The Reading Teacher, 55*(1), 64-69.

Polikoff, M. S. (2012). Instructional alignment under No Child Left Behind. *American Journal of Education, 118*(3), 341-368.

Spillane, J. P. (2004). *Standards deviation: How schools misunderstand education policy.* Cambridge, MA: Harvard University Press.

Tierney, R., & Shanahan, T. (1996). Research on the reading writing relationship. In R. Barr, M. Kamil, P. Mosenthal, & P. D. Pearson (Eds.), *Handbook of reading research 2* (pp. 246–274). Mahwah, NJ: Lawrence Erlbaum.

Todaro, S. A., Millis, K. K., & Dandotkar, S. (2010). The impact of semantic and causal relatedness and reading skill on standards of coherence. *Discourse Processes, 47*, 421-446.

Wiggins, G. (2005). *Understanding by design.* Alexandria, VA: Association for Supervision & Curriculum Development (ASCD).

Vygotsky, L. S. (1978). *Mind in society: The development of higher psychological processes.* Cambridge, MA: Harvard University Press.

Zwiers, J. (2005). *Building reading comprehension habits in grades 6–12.* Newark, DE: International Reading Association.

ABOUT THE AUTHOR

Rozlyn Linder, Ph.D., is the author of The Common Core Guidebook, 6-8: Informational Text Lessons. Rozlyn is a highly sought-after presenter. Known for her energetic, fast-paced seminars and workshops, she has traveled throughout the United States to collaborate with teachers at national and state conferences on literacy. An award-winning teacher, she has taught at all levels from elementary through college. She is passionate about motivating students through explicit instruction and the development of standards-based classrooms. Rozlyn and her husband, Chris, have two spirited daughters.